D0021615

NURTURING FAITH THROUGH THE BOOK OF MORMON

Sidney B. Sperry

Other volumes in the Sperry Symposium Series
from Deseret Book Company:

The Apostle Paul: His Life and His Testimony

Thy People Shall Be My People

The Heavens Are Open

Doctrines of the Book of Mormon

The Lord of the Gospels

A Witness of Jesus Christ

Doctrines for Exaltation

NURTURING FAITH THROUGH THE BOOK OF MORMON

THE 24TH ANNUAL SIDNEY B. SPERRY SYMPOSIUM

DESERET BOOK COMPANY
SALT LAKE CITY, UTAH

Library of Congress Cataloging-in-Publication Data

Sperry Symposium (24th : 1995 : Brigham Young University)
Nurturing faith through the Book of Mormon : the 24th annual Sidney B. Sperry Symposium.
p. cm.
Includes bibliographical references and index.
ISBN 1-57345-159-2
1. Book of Mormon—Congresses. I. Title.
BX8627.S773 1995
289.3'22—dc20 95-46999
CIP

Printed in the United States of America

10 9 8 7 6 5 4 3 2 1

CONTENTS

PREFACE

The twenty-fourth annual Sidney B. Sperry Symposium was held in the Joseph Smith Building Auditorium on the campus of Brigham Young University on 7 October 1995. Because this year marks the one hundredth anniversary of Sidney Sperry's birth and because the conference centered on the Book of Mormon, a scripture that Sperry revered and studied intently, we thought it appropriate to pay special honor to Dr. Sperry by asking prominent Book of Mormon scholars to present papers on important themes, mostly of doctrinal import, in this sacred volume. Their presentations, with some necessary refinements and adjustments to accord with a reading audience, appear in this book.

Besides being recognized authorities on the Book of Mormon text, the authors share other commonalities. All but one served as dean of Religious Education at BYU. All but two taught alongside Brother Sperry. All of them, without exception, gratefully claim his influence in their individual scholarly pursuits.

The foreword is a tribute to Brother Sperry by Ellis T. Rasmussen, a prominent Old Testament scholar and a long-time student of Dr. Sperry's. Brother Rasmussen, who proudly acknowledges his discipleship to Sperry, writes of his mentor's professional accomplishments and personal characteristics.

The first chapter is by Elder Jeffrey R. Holland of the Quorum of the Twelve Apostles, who was the keynote speaker at the symposium. At the conclusion of his address, Elder Holland bore witness to the "eternal Christ, who with his Father gave us the Book of Mormon." Elder Holland's chapter is a poignant and profound study of the premortal Christ as revealed in the Book of Mormon in general and in the encounter between the Savior and the brother of Jared in particular. It is an essay that clearly constitutes a significant contribution to Book of Mormon Christology. Elder Holland declares that like the brother of Jared, that most remarkable of prophets, we too, "ordinary men with ordinary challenges, can rend the veil of unbelief and enter the realms of eternity."

In his thoroughly documented treatise on the house of Israel, Daniel H. Ludlow concludes that by the time of his death Joseph Smith knew more about the destiny and course of the house of Israel than any other person. Much of the Prophet Joseph's knowledge, Brother Ludlow claims, was a direct result of his translation of the Book of Mormon.

That we ought to have greater appreciation for the written Book of Mormon record is one of the implicit messages of Robert J. Matthews' chapter. The purposes of the Lord, Brother Matthews states, could not be realized "if the Book of Mormon were not available as a written document, produced in multiple copies and made available to many people, in a language and form they could read and understand."

Robert L. Millet's essay on fallen man is an important study. Citing various Book of Mormon passages, Brother Millet, presently dean of Religious Education at BYU, deftly explains that though we differ from our Christian neighbors in our understanding of the nature of the Fall, we do agree it was an event of consequence and that it "does indeed take a measured toll on all mankind." Brother Millet demonstrates how the Savior's divine assistance is fundamental to overcoming the effects of the Fall as he provides his own set of *R*s—each of which focuses our attention on Christ and his regenerating power.

The concluding chapter of this volume is written by BYU law professor John W. Welch, who, as did Brother Sperry, enjoys searching and publishing evidences in support of the Book of Mormon. Brother Welch convincingly argues that though evidence in and of itself is not sufficient, it does have its place, for it not only complements our faith but more properly enlarges and nourishes it.

The Prophet Joseph Smith called the Book of Mormon "the most correct of any book on earth" and said that a person "would get nearer to God by abiding by its precepts, than by any other book" (*Teachings of the Prophet Joseph Smith,* sel. Joseph Fielding Smith [Salt Lake City: Deseret Book, 1938], 194). It is our hope that the essays in this book will have the effect of getting us nearer to God and of nurturing our faith in the Holy One of Israel of whom the Book of Mormon so eloquently bears witness.

Paul H. Peterson
David F. Boone
David R. Seely

Special Lectures Committee
BYU Religious Education

A TRIBUTE TO SIDNEY B. SPERRY

ELLIS T. RASMUSSEN

Doubtless many of us at Brigham Young University were students of Sidney Branton Sperry, or students of students—perhaps "unto the third and fourth generation," for he taught here for nearly forty years, from 1932 to 1971. He taught thousands more off-campus as a pioneer in extension programs of BYU. He was a pioneer in religious education in other ways, too, in creating a faculty of full-time religious instructors at BYU. His works live on in those of us involved therein.

He believed sincerely that one must learn by study and by faith as much as possible about the history, practices, principles, and doctrines found in the scriptures and the history of the Church to teach and inculcate true principles and practices adequately and clearly in students' minds. He knew it was not realistic to assume that every member of the Church could step into a classroom, no matter at what level, and function effectively as a teacher without proper study and training for such a demanding profession.

His own career in religious education began, in a way, with his missionary service for The Church of Jesus

---

Ellis T. Rasmussen is professor emeritus of ancient scripture and former dean of Religious Education at Brigham Young University.

Christ of Latter-day Saints in the Southern States in 1919 through 1921. By the time he left on his mission, he had already graduated from the University of Utah (1917) with a bachelor's degree in chemistry and geology. He had worked for a year while in school for the U. S. Smelting Company, worked for a further two years as a chemist for the United States Bureau of Metallurgical Research, and served in World War I as a lieutenant in the Army Field Artillery. During World War II he taught mathematics and Morse code on campus for the Air Force ROTC at BYU. That was no mere academic enterprise; "his son Lyman has identified Dr. Sperry as the first person in Utah to make contact by wireless with ships in the Pacific" ("Sidney B. Sperry, Biographical Sketch," in *They Gladly Taught* [Provo: BYU and the Emeritus Club, 1986], 160).

After completing his mission, he and his chosen companion, Eva Lila Braithwaite, were married on 1 September 1921 in the Salt Lake Temple. They moved to Afton, Wyoming, where he taught high school mathematics, chemistry, and physics—and directed the high school choir. He joined in the early development of the Church Educational System at the invitation of Dr. Adam S. Bennion in 1922. He taught seminary in Moroni and American Fork, Utah, and later held seminary and institute classes in Ogden, Utah, and in Pocatello, Idaho, where he remained as the institute director. His university associations with such men as Adam S. Bennion, John A. Widtsoe, James E. Talmage, and Fredrick C. Pack led him to seek ways to supply students with understandable answers to reasonable questions involving faith—and to counter cynicism.

So it was that Sidney Sperry enrolled as a graduate student (with an undergraduate major in science and mathematics) at the University of Chicago Divinity School, laid the necessary groundwork, and earned a master's degree in Old Testament with a minor in Hebrew in 1926. He continued with studies leading to a doctorate at the University of Chicago Oriental Institute in 1931 in Old Testament Languages and Literature. He and his wife and the first children in their growing family persevered during those trying years of study, which included a year of postdoctoral work in biblical archaeology and additional Semitic languages in Jerusalem at the American Schools of Oriental Research in 1931 and 1932.

He came to BYU in 1932 and began teaching Old Testament, biblical Hebrew, New Testament, Book of Mormon, Greek history, Roman history, and mathematics. Later he initiated off-campus lectures in Utah, Idaho, California, Washington, and Alberta, Canada. He went from time to time to do research in Europe and the Near East and directed the first BYU study program in the Holy Land—a program that led later to an extensive travel-study program in Israel and neighboring countries. At BYU he was a distinguished and beloved teacher, counselor, administrator, and friend.

I had undergraduate classes with him in early 1941 and my first graduate work each summer for eight years, with his encouragement, in Old Testament and Hebrew. As director of the BYU Division of Religion (1948–54) and director of Graduate Studies in Religion (1954–59), he invited me and several others to come to BYU as teaching assistants and work on master's degrees, preparing to become the nucleus of the first full-time faculty in religious instruction at BYU.

He has left a great heritage for his family and for a multitude of students and teachers through his teachings, his books, lectures, monographs, lesson manuals, and magazine articles. He drew ideas from his study and experiences in the Near East to help us appreciate both the scriptures from long ago and those that came through latter-day revelation, for he adeptly drew concepts from each to elucidate, interpret, and evaluate the other. In this tribute to him, I have chosen to review some exemplary highlights from my experiences with him and with his published works in the fields in which I knew him best.

OLD TESTAMENT ARCHAEOLOGY

One of Sidney B. Sperry's first published works was a manual for the adult department of the LDS Mutual Improvement Association in 1938. He had earlier worked on programs for educating adults in the LDS Church, so in fulfilling this MIA assignment he saw an opportunity to inform adult Church members about some exotic but valuable facts drawn from archaeology, Near Eastern languages, and history. He frankly sought to enhance our cognizance and appreciation of the treasures in the gospel, the temple ordinances, and all the blessings of salvation. The manual was entitled *Ancient Records Testify in Papyrus and Stone* and was published by the General Boards of the MIA of The Church of Jesus Christ of Latter-day Saints, in Salt Lake City, Utah, in 1938. This work, though long out of print, exemplifies a broad range of his interests. His intent and attitude are shown in his concise Foreword:

"The people of the Church have always been interested in the Scriptures, but unfortunately there is a dearth of literature among us describing the latest findings of Old Testament archaeology—or the discoveries of long ago for that matter. It is true that there are many treatises, technical and popular, written by men not of our faith that are available, but they do not satisfy our particular needs as we should wish. This manual has been written to partly supply that deficiency. . . .

"Considerable space has been devoted to the manner in which cuneiform records throw light on the Old

Testament and help to elucidate many hitherto obscure and little understood points. Modern discoveries in Bible lands bid fair to completely revolutionize our knowledge of the ancient Near East."

Brother Sperry hoped to deepen the faith of Latter-day Saint students of the Old Testament while enlightening them about the many contributions of archaeology—"the science of the treatment of the material remains of the human past" (cited in *Ancient Records Testify,* 15). He provided the uninitiated with an overview of research in Bible lands, including Palestine, Egypt, and Mesopotamia. He told about the ancient languages deciphered and translated during and after the lifetime of the Prophet Joseph Smith. He explained that prophet's contributions from the Egyptian scrolls containing writings from Abraham and Joseph of old, made available to the Church in the mid 1830s. He recommended that Latter-day Saints take an interest in the continuing archaeological findings and publications. He would be delighted to know of the contributions of our BYU scholars working in archaeological and related research in Egypt right now.

Brother Sperry provided brief analyses and evaluations of the content of the book of Abraham. I remember his appreciation of a gem of information in Abraham 2:6–11 about the essence of the mission of Abraham and his literal and spiritual "seed." He felt that information alone would justify entitling the whole volume a "Pearl of Great Price." I have quoted that passage hundreds of times in explaining what a "chosen people" are "chosen" to do: to make known the gospel of salvation to all the families of the earth that all may eventually enjoy the blessings thereof. Brother Sperry felt too that Abraham's revelations of the nature of the priesthood borne by Melchizedek can give Latter-day Saints a better understanding of the responsibilities of bearing that priesthood.

Dr. Sperry recommended careful study in the Book of Abraham of the accounts of divine planning prior to the spiritual and physical creations of the world and all things (see *Ancient Records Testify,* 88 ff.). He knew, of course, that it was not true archaeology that had brought the mummies from their tomb nor their precious scroll into the hands of the Prophet Joseph, for crass commercial motives had probably led to their discovery and display, but he was convinced that divine influence had brought them to the Prophet.

Among the ancient kings whose inscriptions were indeed identified by archaeologists and linguists, much to the delight of Brother Sperry, was Sargon II, an Assyrian king who reigned in the time of Isaiah (Isaiah 20:1). Against that Assyrian Empire the prophet Isaiah had repeatedly warned Israel, as also against the empires of Tiglath Pileser III and Shalmaneser V. Dr. Sperry felt that an outline of the history of the expansion of the Assyrian empire is seen more clearly through archaeologically discovered artifacts and documents and therefore the worth of Isaiah's prophetic warnings becomes more evident to students. He believed that the urgency and importance of heeding prophetic warnings in our day becomes more evident in light of parallels between their times and ours.

In a chapter entitled "Cuneiform Records and Their Bearing on the Old Testament" (*Ancient Records Testify,* 123–35), Brother Sperry was one of the first in the Church to point out values in studying the ancient Babylonian accounts of the Creation, the Fall, and the Flood. Even though they differ markedly in many details from our accounts in Genesis, the book of Abraham, and the book of Moses, they give evidence that accounts of those epochs were likely known from the beginning, as the book of Moses implies, even though variations in the accounts have developed. That in turn helps us appreciate the more dependable, revealed information we have in our Pearl of Great Price books of Moses and Abraham.

He noted contributions of another sort from inscribed clay tablets found in the excavation of Nuzi, an ancient city of upper Mesopotamia, describing the processes of adopting a servant who could become heir of the adoptive parents. It clarified somewhat the statement of Abraham in Genesis 15:2–3, indicating that his steward, Eliezer of Damascus, must become his heir. Dr. Sperry felt that such records dispel assumptions of the "higher critics" that stories of the patriarchs in Genesis were metaphoric legends contrived to attribute notable origins and qualities to the Hebrews (see *Ancient Records Testify,* 151–60). Sperry called attention to a Babylonian account of the birth and preservation of Sargon of Akkad that parallels in many details the biblical account of the birth and preservation of the life of Moses. The bearing of that account upon the historicity of the Exodus account is, admittedly, problematical.

A different contribution was noted by Brother Sperry in the code of laws of Hammurapi (or Hammurabi), discovered and deciphered between 1901 and 1912 at the site of Susa (or Shushan), of the Abrahamic period. Similarities found in that and other codes of laws comparable to those given by the prophet Moses may be explained in part by a statement by Alma, in the Book of Mormon, that "the Lord doth grant unto all nations, of their own nation and tongue, to teach his word, yea, in wisdom, all that he seeth fit that they should have" (Alma 29:8).

Continuing his evaluation of contributions from the cuneiform records, especially the Nuzi clay tablets (see *Ancient Records Testify,* 173–85), Brother Sperry pointed out parallels to the contract between young Jacob and his potential father-in-law, Laban; it elucidates why negotiations and relations proceeded as they did (see Gen. 29–31).

A collection of cuneiform tablets discovered in 1888 by a peasant woman at Tell El Amarna in the Nile Valley about 160 miles above Cairo, and later identified as documents from the time of Ahmenophis IV (Ikh-en-aton), were of great interest to Dr. Sperry. They deal with the period 1411–1358 B.C. and tell about a mysterious people called "Habiru" invading Canaan from the south and east. Dr. Sperry knew scholars of the time who thought the "Habiru" could have been the Hebrews, invading Canaan after the forty years' wandering since their exodus from Egypt. He recognized, of course, that this hypothesis would have some problems.

Cuneiform records from much later (ca. 860–700 B.C.) interested Dr. Sperry also, for they reflected people and events he knew from 1 and 2 Kings. He appreciated confirmation of the historicity of such events, as well as elucidation of details in the accounts; he was delighted that they refuted certain "higher critics" who had proposed the hypothesis that much of Old Testament narrative material is legend and ethnic fiction. He saw in the cruelty of the Assyrians, as recorded in accounts on tablets and monuments of atrocities done to captives and to the bodies of victims, strong reasons why the missionary-prophet Jonah (ca. 790 B.C.) was reluctant to go on a mission to Nineveh the capital of Assyria. Could he preach repentance unto salvation to such leaders and people? And Dr. Sperry found the Assyrian kings' own records enlightening to readers of the prophecy of Nahum, who expressed exultation at the downfall and just punishment of the royalty at Nineveh (see *Ancient Records Testify,* 187 ff.).

Assyrian records on the Black Obelisk of Shalmaneser III depicted to Dr. Sperry the reality of terrors anticipated by the prophetic warnings that Amos directed to northern Israel (see *Ancient Records Testify,* 68–78). He thought it possible that an eclipse of the sun mentioned in the Assyrian records was the same that Amos anticipated, saying (in the words of God), "I will cause the sun to go down at noon, and I will darken the earth in the clear day" (Amos 8:9; *Ancient Records Testify,* 191).

Dr. Sperry noted that Assyrian records confirm the Old Testament account of the destruction of northern Israel and the decimation of Judah—the latter from the Assyrian account of the attack of Sennacherib on Jerusalem at the time of Isaiah and King Hezekiah. Even as the Bible declares, the Assyrian account tacitly confirms that Jerusalem was spared, for the Assyrians did not boast of overthrowing it (see 2 Kings 19:20–37; see *Ancient Records Testify,* 191–98).

As a scholar in biblical studies, Brother Sperry watched with great interest the developments in Bible lands under the British Mandate governing Palestine after World War I. The British issued the Balfour Declaration, favoring the establishment in Palestine of a national home for the Jews, and fostered biblical archaeological research there. They favored the establishment of the Hebrew University, whose first class was graduated in early 1932. He was delighted with the establishment of the Palestine museum, the American Schools of Oriental Research, and the Oriental Institute at the University of Chicago. He was grateful for the philanthropy of John D. Rockefeller, who helped in these developments. Brother Sperry himself studied at each of those institutions.

He followed avidly the deciphering of the Hebrew-like language of the Moabite Stone, with its bearing on Old Testament language and history, and was intrigued by the ancient Hebrew of the Siloam Inscription in Hezekiah's Tunnel and its message. The Lachish Letters, discovered in 1935 and discerned to be Hebrew documents from the times of the Assyrian invasion of Judah, also demonstrated historicity in the accounts in 2 Kings.

From the Ras Shamra tablets, excavated in 1929 after a peasant discovered ruins near the northern part of the coast of the east end of the Mediterranean (the ancient site of Ugarit), Dr. Sperry saw relevance to the Creation account and to some of the Hebrew Psalms, as well as such poetic passages as Isaiah 27:1 and 51:9–10.

Aramaic writings on papyri found on one of the Elephantine Islands of the Nile, near Assuan, about the time of Brother Sperry's birth, disclosed the amazing fact that there was a Jewish colony there during the 400s B.C.; and they even had a temple there. On values to be found in such resources, Dr. Sperry commented:

"The reader may be interested in knowing why the scholar takes so much interest in such short inscriptions. . . . Only by the accumulation of a great many of them can the scholar pursue his investigations of the linguistic phenomena of Hebrew so necessary for a good translation of the Old Testament. The more we know about the ancient Hebrew language and its dialects, the more clearly and accurately can the Old Testament be rendered into modern English" (*Ancient Records Testify*, 222–23).

It is not surprising that Sidney B. Sperry, as a devout Latter-day Saint scholar, saw also our Book of Mormon as a source of confirmation and clarification of the Old Testament. It came from an ancient text, written during and after Old and New Testament times; then after being buried for centuries, it was brought forth and translated just a century before Brother Sperry began his study of these matters. Of it as a source for biblical scholars he said:

> The Book of Mormon is a contribution to the archaeology of the Old and New Testaments; it con-

> tains material of the highest order bearing on the Bible. . . . The Nephite and Lamanite peoples with which it deals were of Hebrew descent and were acquainted with the Hebrew sacred writings. Even the peoples dealt with in the Book of Ether were probably of the same general race as the patriarchal predecessors of the Hebrews and had similar traditions. The first few chapters of the Book of Mormon recount the departure of a Hebrew family of the tribe of Manasseh from Jerusalem at the Lord's command about the year 600 B.C. . . . They were successful in securing a copy [of the Hebrew scriptures] engraved on brass plates that had been preserved and kept up to date in the [ancestral] family of one Laban. . . . These plates were found to contain the five books of Moses, "which gave an account of the creation of the world, and also of Adam and Eve, who were our first parents; and also a record of the Jews from the beginning, even down to the commencement of the reign of Zedekiah, king of Judah; and also the prophecies of the holy prophets, from the beginning, even down to the commencement of the reign of Zedekiah; and also many prophecies which have been spoken by the mouth of Jeremiah" (1 Nephi 5:11–16). [*Ancient Records Testify*, 229–30]

He affirmed with satisfaction that the Book of Mormon confirms the tenets of conservative Old Testament scholars that Moses wrote "the five books of Moses" and that Isaiah wrote the whole of the book of Isaiah, contrary to the opinion of the so-called higher critics. Moreover, Dr. Sperry observed that the Old Testament is replete with prophecies anticipating the Savior, the Redeemer, the Messiah—and that the Book of Mormon confirms and elucidates such Old Testament prophecies.

OLD TESTAMENT CLASSES AND COMMENTARIES

When I decided to finish my first university degree at BYU and came here in January 1941, I became aware of Dr. Sperry's text entitled *The Spirit of the Old Testament* (Salt Lake City: LDS Department of Education, 1940). He declared in the preface that the purpose of this book for use in the Church Educational System was to "focus attention on the religious and devotional aspects of selected Old Testament books rather than on the critical aspects of them. Where questions of Biblical criticism have been dealt with, conservative views have generally been adopted" (*Spirit of the Old Testament,* iii).

I appreciate his stance with regard to the Old Testament, for it is a book often too much maligned, excessively glorified, or otherwise inaccurately or inadequately described. Brother Sperry said, "By the Old Testament we mean that body of literature or collection of Hebrew scriptures which records in form of history, law, prophecy, psalms, and wisdom the relations of God with a covenant people who were descendants of Abraham. . . . The Old Testament may be spoken of as a book of life because it faithfully records and interprets life situations in the long history of a religious people, and simply and effectively presents a revelation of how God works with man" (*Spirit of the Old Testament,* 1).

He explained that "The Old Covenant" would be a better title and a better translation of the Greek and the Latin title for what we call the Old Testament, for, as he quoted from another scholar, it is "primarily the written record of the origin, terms, and history of the solemn agreement which existed between the Israelitish nation and Jehovah" (*Spirit of the Old Testament,* 1). He explained how and why our Lord when here on earth quoted from portions of the "Law, the Prophets, and the Psalms." He helped us as students see why the canonical books of the Old Testament collection have been preserved and perpetuated as scripture while other writings have been relegated to the categories of "apocrypha" and "pseudepigrapha"—valuable too, but not of like value. He exposed many of us for the first time to the great corpus of rabbinic literature, from Midrashim and Targums to Talmud; he agreed with Nephi that "there is none other people that understand the things which were spoken unto the Jews like unto them, save it be that they are taught after the manner of the things of the Jews" (2 Nephi 25:5). He showed us why many ways and words of peoples of the Near East may be foreign and strange to us but commonly known and understood by the great rabbis of postbiblical times. He also appreciated all the more how our latter-day privilege of revelation for our time helps us better understand doctrines long misunderstood or even unknown.

Brother Sperry sensed how the book of Genesis is, indeed, "The Book of Beginnings." He accounted it "one of the great books of mankind. It stands by itself in the whole of our Old Testament and produces the effect of a single great work of *genius*. Gauged by every worthwhile standard it must be reckoned one of the noblest literary and religious monuments ever produced" (*Spirit of the Old Testament,* 18). He rightly evaluated its key functions in scripture: "Unless this book is understood and its spirit captured it is quite impossible, in our opinion, to plumb the marvelous depths of the Old Testament. It constitutes a fine preface to the volume" (*Spirit of the Old Testament,* 19). He felt that, along with a richly symbolic overview of the origins of life and human institutions, Genesis shows how "Israel" is the name not of a conquering nation but of a people with a spiritual mission to the world, for through those who let God prevail in their lives, the mission of Abraham's seed will be accomplished, bringing everlasting blessings to all families of all nations (see *Spirit of the Old Testament,* 22, and fn. 10).

Dr. Sperry perceived divine programming in the birth and preparation of Moses—and divine character in him as he fulfilled his mission. He felt that through a spiritually attuned mind Moses revealed true doctrines, laws, and authority from God for the benefit of Israel and all mankind. In the books of Joshua and Judges, where accounts of the Israelite seizure of Canaan are written with all the horrors of invasion and dispossession of one people by another, the gentleness and sense of justice of Brother Sperry helped us see that a just and loving God would neither foster nor allow such a process except where evils in an existing culture did not justify that culture's being protected and preserved. Only when they were "ripe in iniquity" was the land cursed against them and the next people were blessed "unto their obtaining power over it" (1 Nephi 17:33–38). And Brother Sperry did not hesitate to point out Israel's recurrent cycles of failure to live obediently enough to be protected forever in it; thus in the course of history they themselves were eventually overthrown.

His purposes in writing a book to characterize the "spirit" of the Old Testament led him also to seek and show the essentials of the great literature produced by the poetic prophets and scribes of Israel. He taught that great literature has a great theme or subject, is beautifully expressed in well-suited diction and imagery, and resonates through man's whole being, arousing noble impulses (see *Spirit of the Old Testament,* 52–53).

Through his own study and wide reading in Hebrew, he learned the power of the simplicity of its vocabulary, the richness of its symbols, and the artistic patterns of its literary structure. Such insights enhanced his understanding and appreciation of "the greatness and beauty of the Authorized Version" of the Bible in English (*Spirit of the Old Testament,* 54).

He cautioned his students against trying to categorize the types of literature in the Old Testament simply into the types commonly known in English literature. He urgently admonished reading scriptural literature both silently and orally until its paranomasia and poetic patterns become aesthetically, intellectually, and spiritually familiar and meaningful. After all, there is indeed both beauty and efficiency in the patterns of poetic parallelism of Hebrew poetry even in translation when the translators and readers themselves are literarily sensitive.

To introduce students to some of the values and beauty of the poetic wisdom literature of the Old Testament, a few chapters of his *Spirit of the Old Testament* are devoted to concepts of that which is and is not worthwhile in earth life, according to "Koheleth" (Ecclesiastes) and a sampling of the Proverbs.

A chapter of surprising conciseness then demonstrates the plan and purposes of the book of Job—written by an ancient author who was "beyond all question an individual of superb literary genius and possessed a penetrating, rich, daring, and creative mind" (*Spirit of the Old Testament,* 78). Sperry recognized that the book of Job "offer[s] no final solution to the problem of unmerited suffering in the world," but yet "leaves us to trust in God—in Him who understands the universe" (*Spirit of the Old Testament,* 88, 89).

In two more brief chapters he tells something of the breadth and depth of the book of Psalms, "the greatest book of devotional literature in existence" (*Spirit of the Old Testament,* 90). He identifies and describes various categories of psalms as to form and substance and chooses a sampling of some superb psalms of adoration, reflection, imprecation against evil, penitence, and messianic yearning.

In the remaining chapters of *The Spirit of the Old Testament,* Dr. Sperry analyzed a sampling of both minor and major prophetic books; he later covered all the minor prophetic books in another text, *The Message of the Twelve Prophets* (Independence, Mo.: Zion's Printing and Publishing Co.). He was aware of and grateful for many of the scholarly works already written on those prophets but desired to do a pioneer work in the field as a Latter-day Saint scholar: "During the past century since the organization of the Church of Jesus Christ of Latter-day Saints, no adequate volume on the Old Testament prophets, written by one of our faith has appeared in print. This fact is easy to understand. During the pioneering stage of our sojourn in the West it was not possible to carry on careful and exacting study of the Bible such as had been advocated by Joseph Smith, the prophet-founder of the Church. Not only so, but our people—like others—found the Old Testament prophets hard to understand. Very few individuals versed in Biblical languages and possessing a sufficient knowledge of Bible manners and customs were available to explain to the people what the prophets were attempting to say—at least in terms that were compatible with the spirit of modern revelation" (*Message of the Twelve Prophets,* 3).

Dr. Sperry hoped in this volume on the twelve so-called Minor Prophets to help college students and others interpret and appreciate more of the values in these little-used prophetic gems. He hoped that his acquaintance with them in their original language and his experiences in the land where the authors had lived would enable him to make the messages live for his students. He explained, for example, that the Hebrew word *nabhi,* usually translated "prophet," indicates one who "speaks forth" for, or on behalf of, another. Thus a "prophet" is primarily not one who predicts, as is commonly supposed, but one who is a spokesman. A prophet of God is a spokesman for God. In his estimate, no inspired prophet of God was minor.

Hosea's experience in the infidelity of his wife, recounted in the opening of his book, is understood by Brother Sperry as a historical metaphor for Jehovah's experience with Israel's covenant infidelity. Then he shows how the conditions in Israel described by Hosea parallel moral and religious conditions in our latter-day society. Thus, for their ills and for ours, Hosea prescribed repentance with Jehovah's plan of redemption as the ultimate remedy (see *Message of the Twelve Prophets,* chap. 2).

Joel's apocalyptic anticipations of destruction and redemption were easily identified by Brother Sperry as heralds of events of our time and beyond, because the angel Moroni cited them to Joseph Smith as such (see *Message of the Twelve Prophets,* chap. 3; Joseph Smith–History 1:41).

Amos was called as a farm boy from a little Judean town seven miles south of Bethlehem to go on a mission to the northern tribes of Israel to warn them of rampant social and spiritual ills and to urge them to repent before they lost all hope for salvation. Brother Sperry sometimes related Amos's mission to his own mission experience and that of farm boys he had as companions in the Southern States Mission of the LDS Church. The poetically beautiful Hebrew of Amos has caused many a biblical scholar to doubt that it could have been written by a mere "herdsman and gatherer of sycomore fruit" (Amos 7:14), but such inspired communications seemed possible to Sperry because of his mission experiences and his awe for the inspired language of another "unlearned" prophet, Joseph Smith (see *Message of the Twelve Prophets,* chap. 4).

In the short prophecy of Obadiah (only twenty-one verses on less than one and one-half pages of our Bible),

Sperry saw allusions to the doom of the ancient nation of Edom, as other scholars do; but thanks to latter-day revelations and comments of prophets of this dispensation, he also saw it as a metaphor for the doom of the wicked of the mortal world prior to the founding of the peaceful kingdom of God, which would provide "saviors . . . on mount Zion," fostering salvation for the repentant and justice for all (*Message of the Twelve Prophets,* 90; Obadiah 1:21).

About Jonah and the "fish story," Brother Sperry once joked, "I don't see why it should be thought so incredible that a fish could be prepared miraculously to swallow a prophet, particularly only a minor prophet!" The first Hebrew words I learned were those of the first verse of the book of Jonah. The language of this little book was sufficiently plain that Dr. Sperry used it for our introduction to biblical Hebrew. In our study of its message, he taught us to appreciate its message delivered in a mode different from that of the other books of prophecy; it is delivered as an experience by a prophet rather than a collection of precepts by him. Jonah's being swallowed up for three days and three nights was eventually cited by our Lord himself as a simile for his own death, burial in a tomb for three days and nights, and ultimate resurrection. Thus it became a message of promise: redemption and atonement for all mankind. We learned also that Dr. Sperry and many other students of these Hebrew scriptures admire the lesson taught to the prophet Jonah, that "God's divine grace is universal" and "all men are precious in God's eyes, but acceptable to Him only if their hearts turn toward Him" (*Message of the Twelve Prophets,* 102).

Micah is called by Dr. Sperry a "Prophet of Judgment, Comfort, and Salvation" (*Message of the Twelve Prophets,* 104). In a little book of just over six pages, Micah touched upon many of the vital topics taught also by his great contemporary, Isaiah. But only Micah revealed the place for the birth of the Savior (Micah 5:1–4). He also encapsulated the basic demands of true religion (6:8) and foretold the establishment of a latter-day Zion in "the top of the mountains" (4:1). Dr. Sperry helped students see the transition Micah made from his vision of the birth of the Savior to His latter-day saving and gathering of Israel by citing Micah 5:7–15 as used in 3 Nephi 20:15–16 and 21:12–21—a source not likely to be cited except by an LDS scholar in Old Testament.

Nahum, "Prophet of Nineveh's Doom" (*Message of the Twelve Prophets,* chap. 8) deals ostensibly with the destruction of Assyria in the seventh century before Christ, but that is shown to be a prototype of the coming destruction of all wickedness in the world at the end of time.

Habakkuk's little literary gem, dated by Dr. Sperry to about the same time as Lehi, deals with the old problem of why the wicked often prosper while the righteous suffer and points up the ultimate truth that "the just shall live by his faith" (Habakkuk 2:4); only therein may he survive. Brother Sperry notes that the "just" is the "righteous," and the word rendered "faith" really means "faithfulness" (see *Message of the Twelve Prophets,* 153–54).

Zephaniah is called "Prophet of the Lord's Day of Wrath," and his message is applied by Dr. Sperry both to the Babylonian conquest of Judah and to a period before the end of the world (see *Message of the Twelve Prophets,* chap. 10). It is amazing how many of these brief prophetic books from twenty-five hundred and more years ago have messages for our own times—if we diligently study them, and seek help from such a scholar and writer as Brother Sperry.

Haggai, whose brief book (two pages long) almost no one quotes nowadays, is the report of a prophet called to give inspired impetus to the struggling Judeans who had returned by the grace of the Lord, manifested through Cyrus of Persia, from captivity in Babylon, ca. 530–520 B.C. They were trying to rebuild a city to live in at Jerusalem and a temple to worship in. In encouraging them to increase their humble efforts to build a replacement for the grand temple of Solomon, destroyed seventy years earlier by the Babylonians, Haggai communicated a grand vision of an ultimate temple and the coming of the Messiah (see *Message of the Twelve Prophets,* 186–87). But for readers of the Bible who are not familiar with the ways in which prophets may connect things present with things future—the immediate with the ultimate—it is helpful to turn to someone who can explain it.

Zechariah, a contemporary to Haggai who collaborated with him in encouraging the returning exiles in Jerusalem to work on the second temple, was a prophet with many other messages for his contemporaries and for us (see *Message of the Twelve Prophets,* chap. 12). Dr. Sperry recognized this longest of the minor prophetic books to be perhaps the most difficult to interpret. He devoted more pages of analysis, interpretation, and commentary to it than to any other save Malachi. With scholarly skill he provided linguistic insights, quoted interpretations of other scholars, and testified of his own convictions, particularly on the messianic prophecies, and sustained them with citations from latter-day revelations. Zechariah is a good evidence for Sperry's tenet that there are no "minor" prophets.

As we have noted, Malachi and Zechariah are the two books in the collection upon which Dr. Sperry left us the longest commentary in *The Message of the Twelve Prophets*. Under the aegis of his interest and guidance I eventually did as my master's thesis a study of "Textual Parallels to the Doctrine and Covenants and Book of Commandments as Found in the Bible" (1951, Brigham

Young University, Provo, Utah), and it was no surprise to him that a higher proportion of phrases of the book of Malachi have counterparts in the Doctrine and Covenants than do any other book in the Bible.

He entitled the last chapter of *The Message of the Twelve Prophets,* "Malachi—Prophet to the Sons of Levi Past and Present." Malachi's little book is full of admonishments good for his times and good for ours—as made evident by Brother Sperry. He showed how significant it is that the Lord himself repeated to Nephi some of the same revelations he had given to Malachi (see *Message of the Twelve Prophets,* 230, and fn. 8; 3 Nephi 24; 25). Brother Sperry also pointed out that latter-day revelation (e.g., D&C 128:24, 39; 84:31–34) identifies latter-day "sons of Levi" (including "sons of Moses" and "sons of Aaron") not necessarily as lineal descendants but as heirs to priesthood keys and responsibilities (see *Message of the Twelve Prophets,* 243–46). He observed that the teachings of Malachi concerning brotherhood among peoples, fidelity in marriage, and faithfulness in tithes and offerings are much needed in our generation.

After his commentary on the Minor Prophets was published, Dr. Sperry continued expanding on it and on his comments about two of the Major Prophets, as first published in his *Spirit of the Old Testament* (chaps. 17–18, 20). Thus he was soon ready to publish a more complete work, *The Voice of Israel's Prophets* (Salt Lake City: Deseret Book, 1952), covering all four of the Major Prophets and the twelve Minor Prophets, when his volume on the latter went out of print.

Dr. Sperry was perfectly cognizant that those sixteen men were not all of the prophets of the Old Testament period. He knew that the Jewish canon of the holy scriptures, which we call the Old Testament, is called the Law, the Prophets, and the Writings; in it, the Prophets embraced both former prophets (covered within the books of Joshua, Judges, Samuel and the Kings) and latter prophets, whose works we call the major and the minor prophetic books. Dr. Sperry also pointed out that latter-day revelations identify prophets from Adam's time to the time of Moses (*Voice of Israel's Prophets,* chap. 1; D&C 107:53–57; Moses 6:22, 23; 7:65, 66; 8:3, 13; Jacob 4:4–6). In this book he sought to do with all sixteen books of the writing prophets what he had done with the twelve books of the Minor Prophets—recognizing that "their writings, unfortunately, are for most people difficult to understand . . . even for those who have a good knowledge of the gospel, not to mention a fair understanding of ancient Oriental history and languages. In these pages I try to take the reader on a personally conducted tour through the mazes of some of the more important prophetic writings" (*Voice of Israel's Prophets,* v).

Neither time nor space will permit anything like a detailed characterization of Brother Sperry's work on the four Major Prophets. With apologies, therefore, I submit only a brief statement of some of my memories about Brother Sperry's contributions to my appreciation of the books of Isaiah, Jeremiah, Ezekiel, and Daniel.

I remember that he spoke of Isaiah as "the dean of the prophets." Indeed, he considered him "one of the greatest men of all time" in artistic capacity for poetic language, in judgment and perception, in courage to defend the right with spiritual intuition and insight. I am often moved to read aloud Isaiah's beautifully expressed prophecies about latter-day Zion; the prophetic call and charge of Isaiah; the anticipations of the birth, works, and majesty of the Messiah; the millennial time of peace to come; the origins and presumptions of the adversary; the great gifts of redemption and atonement; and the visions of the Lord as Creator, Redeemer, and King (see *Voice of Israel's Prophets,* 14; Isaiah 1–2; 6–7; 9; 11; 14;

19:23–25; 25:8–9; 26:19–20; 40–45; 49; 52–53; 58; 65–66).

Dr. Sperry was convinced it would be good, surely, if many Latter-day Saints could know and enjoy more of Isaiah's prophecies than merely those in chapters 2 and 29 (about Zion in the top of the mountains and the book to be brought forth from the dust). Dr. Sperry's book can still help many readers to do so and to solve some of the difficulties they experience with language or literature, background or application.

Jeremiah's mission occurred about a century after Isaiah's. Dr. Sperry believed that understanding the historical setting in which each prophet lived and worked is vital in understanding the warnings and teachings offered. He set the historical stage to help us appreciate the need for such prophets as Jeremiah and Lehi when Babylonian expansion threatened the Near East (ca. 630–580 B.C.). It was a time when the last of the chosen people in Israel were becoming faithless and obdurate, unresponsive to the pleading of the Lord and his prophet. It was therefore a time of suffering and sorrow for the sensitive Jeremiah, and he wept for his people. It was a time of injustice and abuse by leaders of the people whom the Lord and his prophet sought to save, and Jeremiah lashed out at those leaders, especially, for their insensitivity. Jeremiah's book, written for him by his faithful scribe Baruch, includes biographical sketches showing poignant details of the daily life of the prophet at work in the midst of dangers in Jerusalem and in his home city of Anathoth, in the king's court, and in a dungeon prison there.

The account of the mission of the prophet Lehi, related in the early chapters of the Book of Mormon from the same period as the early chapters of Jeremiah, enabled Brother Sperry to make the prophecies of both even more rich in their meaning and more impressive in their vigor. It was advantageous for Dr. Sperry to be a scholar well equipped in faith as well as knowledge, well instructed by prophets living as well as dead. He had rare capacity as a scholar to grasp and take literally the account of the divine call and appointment of Jeremiah, understanding such doctrines as premortal life and foreordination, and able to enlighten fellow scholars and students thereon (see *Voice of Israel's Prophets,* chaps. 11–13).

The breadth and depth of Jeremiah's prophetic horizons concerning God's errant chosen people, their contemporary neighbors, and the future nations of the area and the world, including our world of the latter days, were well perceived by Dr. Sperry. His classroom teaching and his writings enlightened many and will continue to do so in the century after his life.

Ezekiel, "the Prophet of Judah's Captivity" (see *Voice of Israel's Prophets,* chaps. 14–16), was the inspired writer of a book in the sixth century before Christ. It was barely canonized by 200 B.C. and was questioned for centuries thereafter by some Jewish teachers who felt some of its teachings contravened those of Moses and that some of its apocalyptics were too obscure. But Dr. Sperry relished all the truths as revealed in Ezekiel's visions, finding that the doctrines were not only confirmatory of Moses overall but also that the most dubious (to early synods) are indeed harmonious with latter-day revelations (e.g., Ezekiel 18; compare Deuteronomy 24:16; Article of Faith 2). Dr. Sperry saw in the book of Ezekiel vital warnings from a prophet already in captivity in Babylon to fellow Judeans not yet taken captive, for Ezekiel sent messages to them of scathing rebuke and poignant persuasion. But, like other prophets of Israel, he knew his warnings would not generally be heeded, and he predicted dire results to come. Ezekiel also knew and prophetically predicted the return of Judah from Babylon for a time; then later Judah would experience a more complete exile, followed by a latter-day restoration.

With his background in the Book of Mormon, Brother Sperry saw that Ezekiel was inspired to predict the migration of such a colony as Lehi's to the western hemisphere and its establishment there (Ezekiel 17). In Ezekiel 37, partly known to most Latter-day Saints, Brother Sperry saw predictions of the gathering of Israel and Judah and their restoration as one people, as well as the joining of the sacred records from both. Dr. Sperry pointed out Ezekiel's marvelous details of the Lord's latter-day temple in Jerusalem, the place of the Messiah therein, and the distribution of latter-day representatives of all the tribes of Israel in both old and new promised lands (Ezekiel 40–48).

Students of Sidney B. Sperry learned well that the value of the Old Testament prophetic books to Latter-day Saints is not only a few nuggets of prophetic prediction here and there but also hundreds of details—some neglected, though plain, and some obscure but understandable, like gold dust awaiting faithful and diligent discovery and study.

Daniel was recognized as a prophet by Dr. Sperry; indeed, he entitled chapters about him "Daniel, Prophet-Statesman of the Babylonian Captivity" (*Voice of Israel's Prophets,* chaps. 17, 18). It was well-known to him that all but the most conservative scholars consider the book of Daniel a combination of folk stories and imaginative apocalyptic literature. In the Jewish canon the book is not even placed among those of the Prophets—former or latter, major or minor—but among the Writings, along with Job, Psalms, Proverbs, and so forth. Brother Sperry was doubly persuaded that Daniel was an important character in holy writ and the author of an important book that teaches much by example as well as revelation. He held that opinion because of the lack of hard historical evidence to the contrary and because of good confirmatory evidence both in the New Testament and in latter-day revelations. He felt that again and again "Daniel demonstrated the power of faith and prayer in the affairs of men" in his accounts of his own activities and those of his companions in the Babylonian and Median courts (*Voice of Israel's Prophets,* 241–43, 247, 248).

Some scholars have pointed to a lack of logical historical sequencing and the presence of historical anomalies in all existing versions of the book of Daniel; but Dr. Sperry found satisfactory rationales both for the order of items in the collection and for the historical abridging (see *Voice of Israel's Prophets,* 252). Moreover, he accepted the benefit of latter-day prophetic commentary regarding apocalyptic figures and their significance, making the book of Daniel a valuable source for latter-day enlightenment by its precepts as well as its examples. He did, however, wisely warn our people "against making of Chapter 11 a phantasmagoria of fanciful allusions, among which appear pell-mell Ishmael, Rome, Kaiser Wilhelm, Hitler, and the Antichrist. For aught we know, some of these or all of them may have been seen by Daniel, but we cannot prove it" (*Voice of Israel's Prophets,* 268–69).

Brother Sperry perceived in Daniel's vision of the seventy weeks a clear prophecy of the coming of the Savior, his atoning sacrifice, and the subsequent destruction of Jerusalem by the Romans; and he knew that the vision of the stone cut out of the mountain without hands, rolling forth to fill all the earth, is a prophecy of the setting up of the Lord's kingdom on earth in the last days (see *Voice of Israel's Prophets,* 246–48). For him and for any of us who will study it, the book of Daniel is properly among the Major Prophets.

SIDNEY B. SPERRY'S MANY OTHER CONTRIBUTIONS

Though I have paid tribute to Dr. Sperry in the fields wherein I knew him best, I am aware of his many other books and writings not mentioned herein. Indeed, I have read and used most of them and have many on my library shelves where I can still use them. I feel less conscience stricken for not even listing them here because an excellent special issue of the *Journal of Book of Mormon Studies* (4, no. 1) has been published by the Foundation for Ancient Research and Mormon Studies (FARMS); it makes available again significant excerpts from Sperry's *Our Book of Mormon,* provides reprints of many others of his Book of Mormon studies, and concludes with a ten-page bibliography of all of his books, pamphlets, and articles. It also gives chapter titles from each of his major Book of Mormon books as well as his early work, *Ancient Records Testify in Papyrus and Stone.* Notable also in the bibliography are two other volumes Dr. Sperry wrote, which I have not mentioned in this tribute, and which demonstrate how broad his field of interest and his area of expertise really were: *Paul's Life and Letters* (Salt Lake City: Bookcraft, 1955) and *Doctrine and Covenants Compendium* (Salt Lake City: Bookcraft, 1960). I have used them and treasured them for many years.

How did he acquire so much knowledge and produce so many learned works while earning his graduate degrees, being a good family man, and fulfilling his professional roles in teaching and administrative work? His "word processor" of choice as an author was a pencil; and it was a marvel to his publishers that when he had finished a work very little editing and almost no rewriting was needed. I remember someone's calling him "One-Write Sperry."

He and his devoted wife raised a large family of eight good boys and girls, and to that mission alone he gave much time and love. He also loved music and was good at playing both the piano and organ (his instructor in organ was Tabernacle organist John J. McClellan). He served in the Church sometimes as organist, for many years as teacher and defender of the faith, and finally as a patriarch.

How indeed did he do so much and produce so well? It was, no doubt, through his combination of intelligence, avid interest and intellectual curiosity, inspiration and devotion, and a sincere and practical commitment to producing something useful for others. May many continue to enjoy the fruits of his labors in the second century since his birth.

CHAPTER ONE

RENDING THE VEIL OF UNBELIEF

JEFFREY R. HOLLAND

If one were to ask a casual reader of the Book of Mormon to name the principal character in that book, the responses would undoubtedly vary. For one thing, any record covering more than a thousand years of history—with all the persons such a history would include—is unlikely to have any single, central figure emerge over such an extended period as the principal character. Nonetheless, after acknowledging that limitation, perhaps some might list any one of several favorite, or at least memorable, persons. Such names as Mormon, the abridger for whom the book is named, or Nephi, the book's early and very recognizable young prophet, or Alma, to whom so many pages are devoted, or Moroni, the fearless captain who flew the Title of Liberty, or his namesake who concluded the book and delivered it some fourteen hundred years later to the young Joseph Smith—these would undoubtedly be among some of those figures mentioned.

All of these responses would be provocative, but they would also be decidedly incorrect. The principal and

Elder Jeffrey R. Holland, formerly dean of Religious Education and president of Brigham Young University, is a member of the Quorum of the Twelve Apostles of The Church of Jesus Christ of Latter-day Saints.

commanding figure in the Book of Mormon, from first chapter to last, is the Lord Jesus Christ, of whom the book is truly "another testament." From the first page—indeed, from the book's title page—to the last declaration in the text, this testament reveals, demonstrates, examines, and underscores the divine mission of Jesus Christ as recorded in the sacred accounts of two New World dispensations, accounts written for the benefit of a third dispensation, the last and greatest of all dispensations, the dispensation of the fulness of times. This sacred record, written by prophets and preserved by angels, was written for one crucial, fundamental, eternally essential reason: "to the convincing of the Jew and Gentile that Jesus is the Christ, the Eternal God, manifesting himself unto all nations" (Book of Mormon, title page).

In a remarkable vision recorded early in the Book of Mormon, the young prophet Nephi sees the eventual preparation and circulation of the Holy Bible, "a record of the Jews, which contains the covenants of the Lord, which he hath made unto the house of Israel" (1 Nephi 13:23). But, alarmingly, he also sees the abuse and doctrinal decimation of that book as it moves down through the ages and passes through many hands.

It was foretold in this vision that the Bible record would be clear and untarnished in the meridian of time, that in its beginning "it contained the fulness of the gospel of the Lord," with both Old and New Testaments going "from the Jews in purity unto the Gentiles" (1 Nephi 13:24–25). But over time, both through innocent error and malicious design, many doctrines and principles, especially those emphasizing covenantal elements of "the gospel of the Lamb" were lost—and sometimes were simply willfully expunged—from "the book of the Lamb of God" (1 Nephi 13:26, 28). Unfortunately, these missing elements were both "plain and precious"—plain, we presume, in their clarity and power and ability to be understood; precious surely in their profound worth, gospel significance, and eternal importance (1 Nephi 13:28). Whatever the reason for or source of the loss of these truths from the biblical record, that loss has resulted in "pervert[ing] the right ways of the Lord, . . . blind[ing] the eyes and harden[ing] the hearts of the children of men" (1 Nephi 13:27). In painful understatement, "an exceedingly great many do stumble" (1 Nephi 13:29). Honest women and men are less informed of gospel truths and less secure in the salvation of Christ than they deserve to be because of the loss of vital truths from the biblical canon as we have it in modernity (see 1 Nephi 13:21–29).

But in his love and foreknowledge, the great Jehovah, the premortal Christ, promised Nephi, and all who have received Nephi's record, that "after the Gentiles do stumble exceedingly, because of the most plain and precious parts of the gospel of the Lamb which have been kept back . . . I will be merciful unto the Gentiles in that day, insomuch that I will bring forth unto them, in mine own power, much of my gospel, which shall be plain and precious, saith the Lamb.

"For, behold, saith the Lamb: I will manifest myself unto thy seed, that they shall write many things which I shall minister unto them, which shall be plain and precious. . . .

"And in them shall be written my gospel, saith the Lamb, and my rock and my salvation" (1 Nephi 13:34–36).

This promised record, now known to the world as the Book of Mormon, along with "other books" that have now come forth by the revelatory power of the Lamb "shall make known the plain and precious things which have been taken away from [the Bible]; and shall make known to all kindreds, tongues, and people, *that the*

Lamb of God is the Son of the Eternal Father, and the Savior of the world; and that all men must come unto him, or they cannot be saved. And they must come according to the words which shall be established by the mouth of the Lamb; and the words of the Lamb shall be made known in the records of thy seed, as well as in [the Bible]; wherefore they both shall be established in one; for there is one God and one Shepherd over all the earth" (1 Nephi 13:39–41; emphasis added).

Surely the most plain and precious of all truths lost from the Bible, particularly the Old Testament, are the clear, unequivocal, and extensive declarations regarding the coming of Christ and the eternal, essential covenantal elements of his gospel which have been taught beginning with Adam and continuing on down in each dispensation of time. Thus the highest and most revered purpose of the Book of Mormon is to restore to Abraham's seed that crucial message declaring Christ's divinity, convincing all who read its pages with "a sincere heart and real intent" that Jesus is the Christ (see Moroni 10:4).

The fact that four-fifths of this record comes out of a period *before* Christ's birth, the fact that it is a record of an otherwise unknown people, the fact that inspiring insights and deep doctrines regarding Jesus are revealed here and found nowhere else in the biblical canon—or all of Christendom, for that matter—and the fact that the Book of Mormon reaffirms the truthfulness and divinity of that Bible insofar as the latter has been translated correctly are just a few of the reasons that the book should rightly be considered the most remarkable and important religious text produced since the New Testament gospels were compiled nearly two millennia ago. Indeed, in light of the plain and precious portions which have been lost from the New Testament as well as the Old Testament, it could be said that in restoring ancient biblical truths and adding scores of new ones about the Only Begotten Son of the Living God of us all, the Book of Mormon links with the Holy Bible to form in that union the most remarkable and important religious texts ever given to the world in any age of time.

The Book of Mormon has many purposes and it contains many true and stimulating principles, but one purpose transcends all others in both kind and degree. That purpose is "the convincing of the Jew and Gentile that Jesus is the Christ" (Book of Mormon, title page).

A very special contribution the Book of Mormon makes in this matter is to our knowledge of the *premortal* Christ. Christ as Jehovah, Christ as the God of Lehi and Nephi and the brother of Jared before His birth as well as the Redeemer of Mormon and Moroni after it, is one of the prominent messages of this record.

In modern times many students of religion have great difficulty in linking Old Testament theology and divinity with that which is presented in the New Testament. The Book of Mormon does so very much to bridge that gap, not only in terms of actual history, beginning six hundred years before Christ and ending four hundred years afterward, but also in the continuity of doctrine and consistent image of divinity that is taught through that period. We talk about the two sticks of Judah and Joseph coming together, as prophesied by Ezekiel, as one of the great latter-day contributions of the Book of Mormon (see Ezekiel 37:15–28); however, I think it is nearly as important to note, in bringing "sticks" together, what the Book of Mormon does to unite the Old Testament with the New Testament in a way that is not recognized or sometimes even seen as a possibility in other religious traditions.

Nephi, Jacob, and Isaiah—all living and prophesying before Christ—are positioned where they are at the beginning of the book to serve as the three ancient witnesses of the Book of Mormon or, more specifically, three special Book of Mormon witnesses of Christ, which surely they are. But that role of witness is shared by many, many others in the Book of Mormon, most of them prior to Christ's birth and ministry in mortality.

Amulek says to his fellow citizens of Ammonihah (about 74 B.C.): "My brethren, I think that it is impossible that ye should be ignorant of the things which have been spoken concerning the coming of Christ, who is taught by us to be the Son of God; yea, *I know that these things were taught unto you bountifully* before your dissension from among us" (Alma 34:2; emphasis added).

The coming of Christ and the particulars of his mission and message were taught bountifully throughout the entire course of the Book of Mormon. It should not be surprising that the book as we now have it begins with a vision of "One descending out of the midst of heaven, and he beheld that his luster was above that of the sun at noon-day" (1 Nephi 1:9). This vision of the premortal Christ, accompanied in spirit by "twelve others," brought forth a book in which Lehi was bidden to read. The book spoke of "many great and marvelous things," including the plain declaration "of the coming of a Messiah, and also the redemption of the world" (1 Nephi 1:14, 19).

From these opening passages onward, the Book of Mormon speaks continually of Christ before his mortal birth, during his sojourn both among the Jews and the Nephites, and in his postmortal rule and reign in the eternities that follow. Even though his contemporaries in Jerusalem rejected that message given by Lehi, that great prophet nevertheless continued his prophecies of "a Messiah, or, in other words, a Savior of the world" (1 Nephi 10:4). Included in Lehi's very specific knowledge of the coming of Christ to mortality were such revelatory details as a vision that the Messiah would be slain and "should rise from the dead, and should make himself manifest, by the Holy Ghost, unto the Gentiles" (1 Nephi 10:11).

Whether it was this kind of revelation or something even more definitive (a personal appearance of Christ?) we do not know, but Lehi obviously had some very special manifestations regarding the Son of God. Shortly before his death, he testified to his sons: "Behold, the Lord hath redeemed my soul from hell; *I have beheld his glory,* and I am encircled about eternally in the arms of his love" (2 Nephi 1:15; emphasis added).

As early as Nephi's writings we learn the name which the Messiah shall carry, but that same Nephi is quick to acknowledge that other ancient prophets knew the name as well. "For according to the words of the prophets," he writes, "the Messiah cometh in six hundred years from the time that my father left Jerusalem; and according to the words of the prophets, and also the word of the angel of God, his name shall be Jesus Christ, the Son of God" (2 Nephi 25:19).

Nephi's brother Jacob follows that acknowledgment with a powerful testimony of the breadth of revelation and widespread knowledge of Christ that had been given to those ancient prophets. He wrote: "For this intent have we written these things, that they may know that we knew of Christ, and we had a hope of his glory many hundred years before his coming; and not only we ourselves had a hope of his glory, but also all the holy prophets which were before us.

"Behold, they believed in Christ and worshiped the Father in his name, and also we worship the Father in his name. And for this intent we keep the law of Moses, it pointing our souls to him. . . .

"Wherefore, we search the prophets, and we have many revelations and the spirit of prophecy; and having all these witnesses we obtain a hope, and our faith becometh unshaken, insomuch that we truly can command in the name of Jesus and the very trees obey us, or the mountains, or the waves of the sea" (Jacob 4:4–6).

In that bold and persuasive spirit he pleads with his brethren: "Behold, will ye reject these words? Will ye reject the words of the prophets; and will ye reject all the words which have been spoken concerning Christ, after so many have spoken concerning him; and deny the good word of Christ, and the power of God, and the gift of the Holy Ghost, and quench the Holy Spirit, and make a mock of the great plan of redemption, which hath been laid for you?" (Jacob 6:8–9).

But soon enough one came doing exactly those things, Sherem, the first of the anti-Christs in the Book of Mormon. Sherem came declaring "that there should be no Christ" and in every way attempted to "overthrow the doctrine of Christ" (Jacob 7:2). Knowing that Jacob "had faith in Christ who should come," Sherem sardonically made particular effort to confront and challenge him on the practice of what Sherem called "preaching that which ye call the gospel, or the doctrine of Christ" (Jacob 7:3, 6). His argument was based on the feeble and tediously predictable reasoning of all anti-Christs—that "no man knoweth of such things; for he cannot tell of things to come" (Jacob 7:7).

Of Sherem, Jacob asks: "Believest thou the scriptures? And he said, Yea. And I said unto him: Then ye do not understand them; for they truly testify of Christ. Behold, I say unto you that none of the prophets have written, nor prophesied, save they have spoken concerning this Christ" (Jacob 7:10–11).

One of the greatest of those prophets in the Book of Mormon—indeed, a very strong case could be made for calling him *the* greatest of the prophets in the Book of Mormon—goes unnamed in the record that documents

Christ's remarkable life. That prophet is identified to the modern reader only as "the brother of Jared." Yet even in such near anonymity, the revelation that unfolded before this man's eyes was so extraordinary that his life and legacy to us have become synonymous with bold, consummate, perfect faith.

In the dispersion required of them at the time of the Tower of Babel, the people of Jared arrived at "the great sea which divideth the lands" (Ether 2:13) where they pitched their tents, awaiting further revelation regarding the crossing of a mighty ocean. For four years they awaited divine direction, but apparently they waited too casually—without supplication and exertion. Then this rather remarkable moment presented itself:

"And it came to pass at the end of four years that the Lord came again unto the brother of Jared, and stood in a cloud and talked with him. And for the space of three hours did the Lord talk with the brother of Jared, and chastened him because he remembered not to call upon the name of the Lord" (Ether 2:14).

It is difficult to imagine what a three-hour rebuke from the Lord might be like, but the brother of Jared endured it. With immediate repentance and immediate prayer, this prophet once again sought guidance for the journey they had been assigned and for those who were to pursue it. God accepted his repentance and lovingly gave further direction for this crucial mission.

For such an oceanic crossing these families and their flocks needed seaworthy crafts similar to the barges they had constructed for earlier water travel—small, light, dish-shaped vessels identical in design above and beneath so that they were capable of staying afloat even when facing overwhelming waves or, worse yet, when they might be overturned by them. These "exceedingly tight" crafts (Ether 2:17) were obviously boats of unprecedented design and undiminished capability, made under the direction of him who ruled the seas and the winds that rend them to the end that the vessels might travel with the "lightness of a fowl upon the water" (Ether 2:16).

These were miraculously designed and meticulously constructed ships. But they had one major, seemingly insoluble limitation. In such a tight, seaworthy design, there was no means of allowing light for the seafarers who would travel in them. "The brother of Jared . . . cried again unto the Lord saying: O Lord, behold I have done even as thou hast commanded me; and I have prepared the vessels for my people, and behold there is no light in them. Behold, O Lord, wilt thou suffer that we shall cross this great water in darkness?" (Ether 2:21–22).

Then comes an extraordinary and unexpected response from the Creator of heaven and earth and all things that in them are, he who boldly declared to Abraham, "Is anything too great for the Lord?" (Genesis 18:14).

"And the Lord said unto the brother of Jared: *What will ye that I should do* that ye may have light in your vessels?" (Ether 2:23; emphasis added). Then, as if such a disarming inquiry from omnipotent Deity is not enough, the Lord proceeds to verbalize the very problems that the brother of Jared already knows only too well.

"For behold, ye cannot have windows, for they will be dashed in pieces; neither shall ye take fire with you, for ye shall not go by the light of fire.

"For behold, ye shall be as a whale in the midst of the sea; for the mountain waves shall dash upon you. . . . *Therefore what will ye that I should prepare for you* that ye may have light when ye are swallowed up in the depths of the sea?" (Ether 2:23–25; emphasis added).

Clearly the brother of Jared was being tested. The Lord had done his part—miraculously, profoundly, ingeniously. Unique, resolutely seaworthy ships for crossing the ocean had been provided. The brilliant engineering had been done. The hard part of this construction project was over. Now he wanted to know what the brother of Jared would do about incidentals.

After what was undoubtedly a great deal of soul-searching and head-scratching, the brother of Jared came before the Lord—perhaps red-faced but not empty-handed. In a clearly apologetic tone, he says: "Now behold, O Lord, and do not be angry with thy servant because of his weakness before thee; for we know that thou art holy and dwellest in the heavens, and that we are unworthy before thee; because of the fall our natures have become evil continually; nevertheless, O Lord, thou hast given us a commandment that we must call upon thee, that from thee we may receive according to our desires.

"Behold, O Lord, thou hast smitten us because of our iniquity, and hast driven us forth, and for these many years we have been in the wilderness; nevertheless, thou hast been merciful unto us. O Lord, look upon me in pity, and turn away thine anger from this thy people, and suffer not that they shall go forth across this raging deep in darkness; but behold these things which I have molten out of the rock" (Ether 3:2–3).

Things. The brother of Jared hardly knows what to call them. *Rocks* probably doesn't sound any more inspiring. Here, standing next to the Lord's magnificent handiwork, these ne plus ultra, impeccably designed, and marvelously unique seagoing barges, the brother of Jared offers for his contribution *rocks.* As he eyes the sleek ships the Lord has provided, it is a moment of genuine humility.

He hurries on. "And I know, O Lord, that thou hast all power, and can do whatsoever thou wilt for the benefit of man; therefore touch these stones, O Lord, with thy finger, and prepare them that they may shine forth in darkness; and they shall shine forth unto us in the vessels which we have prepared, that we may have light while we shall cross the sea.

"Behold, O Lord, thou canst do this. We know that thou art able to show forth great power, which looks small unto the understanding of men" (Ether 3:4–5).

For all of his self-abasement, the faith of the brother of Jared is apparent. In fact, we might better say *transparent* in light of the purpose for which these stones will be used. Surely God, as well as the reader, feels something very striking in the childlike innocence and fervor of this man's faith. *"Behold, O Lord, thou canst do this."* Perhaps there is no more powerful, single line of faith spoken by man in scripture. It is almost as if he is encouraging God, emboldening him, reassuring him. Not "Behold, O Lord, I am sure that thou canst do this." Not "Behold, O Lord, thou hast done many greater things than this." However uncertain the prophet is about his own ability, he has *no* uncertainty about God's power. There is nothing here but a single, clear, bold, and assertive declaration with no hint or element of vacillation. It is encouragement to Him who needs no encouragement but who surely must have been touched by it. "Behold, O Lord, thou canst do this."

What happened next ranks among the greatest moments in recorded history, surely among the greatest moments in recorded faith. It establishes the brother of Jared among the greatest of God's prophets forever. As the Lord reaches forth to touch the stones one by one with his finger—a response, it would seem, coming in undeniable response to the commanding faith of the brother of Jared—"the veil was taken from off the eyes of the brother of Jared, and he saw the finger of the Lord; and it was as the finger of a man, like unto flesh and blood; and the brother of Jared fell down before the

Lord, for he was struck with fear" (Ether 3:6).

The Lord, seeing the brother of Jared fall to the earth, commands him to rise and asks, "Why hast thou fallen?" (Ether 3:7).

The reply: "I saw the finger of the Lord, and I feared lest he should smite me; for I knew not that the Lord had flesh and blood" (Ether 3:8).

Then this marvelous declaration from the Lord: "Because of thy faith thou hast seen that I shall take upon me flesh and blood; and never has man come before me with such exceeding faith as thou hast; for were it not so ye could not have seen my finger. Sawest thou more than this?" (Ether 3:9).

The brother of Jared answers, "Nay; Lord, show thyself unto me" (Ether 3:6–10). The Lord removed the veil completely from the eyes of the brother of Jared and came into full view of this resolutely faithful man.

Then this most remarkable revelation of the premortal Jehovah: "Behold, I am he who was prepared from the foundation of the world to redeem my people," he said. "Behold, I am Jesus Christ. I am the Father and the Son. In me shall all mankind have life, and that eternally, even they who shall believe on my name; and they shall become my sons and my daughters.

"And never have I showed myself unto man whom I have created, for never has man believed in me as thou hast. Seest thou that ye are created after mine own image? Yea, even all men were created in the beginning after my own image.

"Behold, this body, which ye now behold, is the body of my spirit; and man have I created after the body of my spirit; and even as I appear unto thee to be in the spirit will I appear unto my people in the flesh" (Ether 3:14–16).

Before examining the doctrinal truths taught in this divine encounter, it will be useful to note two seemingly problematic issues here, issues that would seem to have reasonable and acceptable resolutions.

The first issue is suggested in two questions the Lord asks the brother of Jared during the vision as it unfolds: "Why hast thou fallen?" and "Sawest thou more than this?" It is a basic premise of Latter-day Saint theology that God "knoweth all things, and there is not anything save he knows it" (2 Nephi 9:20). The scriptures, both ancient and modern, are replete with this assertion of omniscience. Nevertheless, God has frequently asked questions of men, usually as a way to test their faith, measure their honesty, or allow their knowledge greater development. For example, he called unto Adam in the Garden of Eden, "Where art thou?" and later asks Eve, "What is this that thou hast done?" (Genesis 3:9, 13), yet an omniscient parent clearly knew the answer to both questions, for he could see where Adam was and he watched what Eve had done. It is obvious that the questions are for the children's sake, giving Adam and Eve the responsibility of replying honestly. Later, in trying Abraham's faith, God repeatedly called out regarding Abraham's whereabouts, to which the faithful patriarch would answer: "Here am I" (Genesis 22:11). The purpose in this scriptural moment was not to provide God with information he already knew but to reaffirm Abraham's fixed faith and unwavering position in the most difficult of all parental tests. These kinds of rhetorical questions are frequently used by God, particularly in assessing faith, honesty, and the full measure of agency, allowing the "students" the freedom and opportunity to express themselves as revealingly as they wish, even though God knows the answer to his own and all other questions.

The second issue that requires preliminary comment stems from the Lord's exclamation, "Never has man come before me with such exceeding faith as thou hast; for were it not so ye could not have seen my finger"

(Ether 3:9). And later, "Never have I showed myself unto man whom I have created, for never has man believed in me as thou hast" (Ether 3:15).The potential for confusion here comes with the realization that many—indeed, we would assume all—of the major prophets living prior to the brother of Jared had seen God. How then does one account for the Lord's declaration? Adam's face-to-face conversations with God in the Garden of Eden can be exempted because of the paradisiacal, prefallen state of that setting and relationship. Furthermore, other prophets' visions of God, such as Moses and Isaiah in the Bible, or Nephi and Jacob in the Book of Mormon, came after this "never before" experience of the brother of Jared. But before the era of the Tower of Babel, the Lord did appear unto Adam and "the residue of his posterity who were righteous" in the valley of Adam-ondi-Ahman three years before Adam's death (see D&C 107:53–55). And we are left with Enoch, who said very explicitly, "I saw the Lord; and he stood before my face, and he talked with me, even as a man talketh one with another, face to face" (Moses 7:4). We assume there would have been other prophets living in the period between Adam's leaving the Garden of Eden and the building of the Tower of Babel who also saw God in a similar manner, including Noah who "found grace in the eyes of the Lord" and "walked with God" (Genesis 6:8–9), the same scriptural phrase used to describe Enoch's relationship with the Lord (see Genesis 5:24).

This issue has been much discussed by Latter-day Saint writers, and there are several possible explanations, any one—or all—of which may cast some light upon the larger truth of this passage. Nevertheless, without additional scriptural revelation or commentary on the matter, any conjecture is only that—conjecture—and as such is inadequate and incomplete.

One possibility is that this is simply a comment made

in the context of one dispensation and as such applies only to the Jaredites and Jaredite prophets—that Jehovah has never before revealed himself to one of their seers and revelators. Obviously this theory has severe limitations when measured against such phrases as "never before" and "never has man" and combined with the realization that Jared and his brother are the fathers of this dispensation, the first to whom God could have revealed himself in their era.

Another suggestion is that the lowercase reference to "man" is the key to this passage, suggesting that the Lord has never revealed himself to the unsanctified, to the nonbeliever, to temporal, earthy, natural man. The implication here is that only those who have put off the natural man, only those who are untainted by the world—in short, the sanctified (such as Adam, Enoch, and now the brother of Jared)—are entitled to this privilege.

Some have believed that the Lord here means he had never before revealed himself to this degree or to this extent. This theory would suggest that divine appearances to earlier prophets had not been with this same "fulness," that never before had the veil been lifted to give such a complete revelation of Christ's nature and being.

A further possibility is that this is the first time Jehovah has appeared and identified himself as Jesus Christ, the Son of God, thus the interpretation of the passage being "never have I showed myself [as Jesus Christ] unto man whom I have created" (Ether 3:15). This possibility is reinforced by one way of reading Moroni's later editorial comment: "Having this perfect knowledge of God, he could not be kept from within the veil; therefore he saw *Jesus*" (Ether 3:20; emphasis added).

Yet another interpretation of this passage is that the

faith of the brother of Jared was so great he saw not only the *spirit* finger and body of the premortal Jesus (which presumably many other prophets had also seen) but also had some distinctly more revealing aspect of Christ's body of flesh, blood, and bone. Exactly what insight into the flesh-and-blood nature of Christ's future body the brother of Jared might have had is not clear, but Jehovah does say to him, "Because of thy faith thou hast seen that I shall take upon me flesh and blood" (Ether 3:9), and Moroni does say that Christ revealed himself in this instance "in the likeness of the same body even as he showed himself unto the Nephites" (Ether 3:17). Some have taken that to mean literally "the same body" the Nephites would see—a body of flesh and blood. A safer position would be that it was at least the exact spiritual likeness of that future body. Jehovah says, "Behold, this body, which ye now behold, is the body of my spirit . . . and even as I appear unto thee to be in the spirit will I appear unto my people in the flesh" (Ether 3:16), and Moroni says, "Jesus showed himself unto this man in the spirit" (Ether 3:17).

A final—and in terms of the faith of the brother of Jared (which is the issue at hand) surely the most persuasive—explanation for me is that Christ is saying to the brother of Jared, 'Never have I showed myself unto man *in this manner, without my volition, driven solely by the faith of the beholder.*' As a rule, prophets are *invited* into the presence of the Lord, are bidden to enter his presence by him and only with his sanction. The brother of Jared, on the other hand, stands alone then (and we assume now) in having thrust himself through the veil, not as an unwelcome guest but perhaps technically an uninvited one. Says Jehovah, *"Never has man come before me with such exceeding faith as thou hast; for were it not so ye could not have seen my finger. . . . Never has man believed in me as thou hast"* (Ether 3:9, 15; emphasis added).

Obviously the Lord himself is linking unprecedented faith with this unprecedented vision. If the vision is not unique, then it has to be the faith—and how the vision is obtained—that is so remarkable. The only way this faith could be so remarkable would be in its ability to take this prophet, uninvited, where others had only been able to go by invitation.

Indeed it would appear that this is Moroni's own understanding of the circumstance, for he later writes, "Because of the knowledge [which has come as a result of faith] of this man *he could not be kept from beholding within the veil*. . . . Wherefore, having this perfect knowledge of God, *he could not be kept from within the veil;* therefore he saw Jesus" (Ether 3:19–20; emphasis added).

This may be one of those very provocative examples (except that it is real life and not hypothetical) about God's power. Schoolboy philosophers sometimes ask, "Can God make a rock so heavy that he cannot lift it?" or "Can God hide an item so skillfully that he cannot find it?" Far more movingly and importantly we may ask here, "Could God have stopped the brother of Jared from seeing through the veil?" At first blush one is inclined to say, "Surely God could block such an experience if he wished to." But think again. Or, more precisely, read again. "This man . . . *could not be kept from beholding within the veil . . . he could not be kept from within the veil*" (Ether 3:19–20; emphasis added).

No, this may be an absolutely unprecedented case of a prophet's will and faith and purity so closely approaching that of heaven's that the man moves from understanding God to being actually like him, with his same thrust of will and faith, at least in this one instance. What a remarkable doctrinal statement about the power of a mortal man's faith! And not an ethereal, unreachable, select category of a man, either. This is one who once forgot to call upon the Lord, one whose best ideas focused on rocks, and one who doesn't even have a traditional name in the book that has immortalized his remarkable feat of faith. Given such a man with such faith, it should not be surprising that the Lord would show this prophet much, show him visions that would be relevant to the mission of all the Book of Mormon prophets and to the events of the latter-day dispensation in which the book would be received.

After the prophet stepped through the veil to behold the Savior of the world, he was not limited in seeing the rest of what the eternal world revealed. Indeed, the Lord showed him "all the inhabitants of the earth which had been, and also all that would be; and he withheld them not from his sight, even unto the ends of the earth" (Ether 3:25). The staying power for such an experience was once again the faith of the brother of Jared, for "the Lord could not withhold anything from him, for he knew that the Lord could show him all things" (Ether 3:26).

This vision of "all the inhabitants of the earth which had been, and also all that would be . . . even unto the ends of the earth" (Ether 3:25) was similar to that given to Moses and other of the prophets (see Moses 1:27–29). In this case, however, it was written down in great detail and then sealed up. Moroni, who had access to this recorded vision, wrote on his plates "the very things which the brother of Jared saw" (Ether 4:4). Then he, too, sealed them up and hid them again in the earth before his death and the final destruction of the Nephite civilization. Of this vision given to the brother of Jared, Moroni wrote, "There never were greater things made manifest than those which were made manifest unto the brother of Jared" (Ether 4:4).

Those sealed plates constitute the sealed portion of the Book of Mormon which Joseph Smith did not translate. Furthermore they will remain sealed, literally as well as figuratively, until "they shall exercise faith in me, saith the Lord, even as the brother of Jared did, that they may become sanctified in me, then will I manifest unto them the things which the brother of Jared saw, even to the unfolding unto them all my revelations, saith Jesus Christ, the Son of God, the Father of the heavens and of the earth, and all things that in them are" (Ether 4:7).

The full measure of this unprecedented and unexcelled vision—"there never were greater things made manifest"—are yet to be made known to the children of men. But consider what was made known in one man's experience in receiving it, consider that the time was approximately two thousand years before Christ's birth, and consider what is *not* presently contained in the Old Testament canon of that period regarding Jehovah and his true characteristics. These twenty-five items are all drawn from Ether 3 and 4:

1. Jehovah, the God of the pre-Christian era, was the premortal Jesus Christ, identified here by that name (see Ether 3:14).

2. Christ is both a Father and a Son in his divine relationship with the children of men (see Ether 3:14).

3. Christ was "prepared from the foundation of the world to redeem [his] people" (Ether 3:14), knowledge which had been shared before with Enoch and later would be shared with John the Revelator (see Moses 7:47; Revelation 13:8).

4. Christ had a spirit body, which looked like and was in the premortal form of his physical body, like "unto flesh and blood," including fingers, voice, face, and all other physical features (Ether 3:6).

5. Christ assisted in the creation of man, fashioning the human family "after the body of my spirit" (Ether 3:16).

6. With a spirit body and the divinity of his calling,

the premortal Christ spoke audibly, in words and language understood by mortals (see Ether 3:16).

7. Christ is a God, acting for and with his Father, who is also a God (see Ether 3:14; 4:7).

8. Christ reveals some truths to some that are to be kept until an appointed time (his "own due time") from others (see Ether 3:24).

9. Christ uses a variety of tools and techniques in revelation, including the interpreting power of "two stones" such as those used in the Urim and Thummim (see Ether 3:23; D&C 17:1).

10. Christ's later atoning, redeeming role is clearly stated even before it has been realized in his mortal life. Furthermore, in a most blessed way for the brother of Jared, it is immediately efficacious. "I am he who was prepared from the foundation of the world to redeem my people," Christ says. "In me shall all mankind have life, and that eternally, even they who shall believe on my name; and they shall become my sons and my daughters" (Ether 3:14).

Then the brother of Jared has his redemption pronounced, as though the Atonement had already been carried out. "Because thou knowest these things ye are redeemed from the fall," Christ promises him, "therefore ye are brought back into my presence; therefore I show myself unto you" (Ether 3:13).

This statement underscores the eternal nature of the Atonement, its effects reaching out to all those who lived before the Savior's birth as well as all those living after it. All who in Old Testament times were baptized in Christ's name had the same claim upon eternal life that the brother of Jared had, even though Christ had not yet even been born. In matters of the Atonement, as in all other eternal promises, "time only is measured unto men" (Alma 40:8).

11. Christ had past knowledge of all the inhabitants

of the earth which had been and foreknowledge of all that would be, showing all of these to the brother of Jared (see Ether 3:25).

Moroni, in recording the experience of the brother of Jared, adds these insights and revelations which come from the same encounter:

12. Future Saints will need to be sanctified in Christ to receive all of his revelations (see Ether 4:6).

13. Those who reject the vision of the brother of Jared will be shown "no greater things" by Christ (Ether 4:8).

14. At Christ's command "the heavens are opened and are shut," "the earth shall shake," and "the inhabitants thereof shall pass away, even so as by fire" (Ether 4:9).

15. Believers in the vision of the brother of Jared will be given manifestations of Christ's spirit. Because of such spiritual experience, belief shall turn to knowledge and those "shall know that these things are true" (Ether 4:11).

16. "Whatsoever thing persuadeth men to do good" is of Christ. Good comes of none except Christ (Ether 4:12).

17. Those who do not believe Christ's words would not believe him personally (see Ether 4:12).

18. Those who do not believe Christ would not believe God the Father who sent him (see Ether 4:12).

19. Christ is the light and the life and the truth of the world (see Ether 4:12).

20. Christ will reveal "greater things" (Ether 4:13), "great and marvelous things" (Ether 4:15), knowledge hidden "from the foundation of the world" (Ether 4:14) to those who rend the veil of unbelief and come unto him.

21. Believers are to call upon the Father in the name of Christ "with a broken heart and a contrite spirit" if they are to "know that the Father hath remembered the

covenant which he made" unto the house of Israel (Ether 4:15).

22. Christ's revelations to John the Revelator will be "unfolded in the eyes of all the people" in the last days, even as they are about to be fulfilled (Ether 4:16).

23. Christ commands all the ends of the earth to come unto him, believe in his gospel, and be baptized in his name (see Ether 4:18).

24. Signs shall follow those that believe in Christ's name (see Ether 4:18).

25. Those faithful to Christ's name at the last day shall be "lifted up to dwell in the kingdom prepared for [them] from the foundation of the world" (Ether 4:19).

Indeed, an appeal like that of the brother of Jared is given by the Father to both Gentile and Israelite, to whom this record is sent. Asking the latter-day reader to pierce the limits of shallow faith, Christ cries:

"Come unto me, O ye Gentiles, and I will show unto you the greater things, the knowledge which is hid up because of unbelief.

"Come unto me, O ye house of Israel, and it shall be made manifest unto you how great things the Father hath laid up for you, from the foundation of the world; and it hath not come unto you, because of unbelief.

"Behold, *when ye shall rend that veil of unbelief* which doth cause you to remain in your awful state of wickedness, and hardness of heart, and blindness of mind, then shall the great and marvelous things which have been hid up from the foundation of the world from you—yea when ye shall call upon the Father in my name, with a broken heart and a contrite spirit, then shall ye know that the Father hath remembered the covenant which he made unto your fathers, O house of Israel" (Ether 4:13–15).

The Book of Mormon is predicated on the willingness of men and women to "rend the veil of unbelief" in order to behold the revelations—and the Revelation—of God (Ether 4:15). It would seem that the humbling experience of the brother of Jared in his failure to pray and his consternation over the sixteen stones were included in this account to show just how mortal and just how normal he was—so very much like the men and women we know and at least in some ways so much like ourselves. His belief in himself and his view of himself may have been limited—much like our view of ourselves. But his belief in God was unprecedented. It was without doubt or limit: "I know, O Lord, that thou hast all power, and can do whatsoever thou wilt for the benefit of man; therefore touch these stones, O Lord, with thy finger" (Ether 3:4).

And from that command given to the Lord, for it does seem to be something of a command, the brother of Jared and the reader of the Book of Mormon would never be the same again. Ordinary individuals with ordinary challenges could rend the veil of unbelief and enter the realms of eternity. And Christ, who was prepared from the foundation of the world to redeem his people, would be standing at the edge of that veil to usher the believer through.

CHAPTER TWO

THE DESTINY OF THE HOUSE OF ISRAEL

DANIEL H. LUDLOW

Following a habit developed in high school and college days when I participated in debate tournaments, I have gone to the dictionary and to concordances of the scriptures to make certain I understood the full ramifications of the major terms in my assigned topic: the *destiny* of the *house of Israel.*

DESTINY

Webster's Third New International Dictionary of the English Language, Unabridged, helped me with the word *destiny.* It contains five different definitions of the word, the basic meaning of which is "that to which any person or thing is destined." Some of the definitions and explanations of the word *destiny* are as follows:

> *1a* predetermined state: condition foreordained by divine will or by human will: unavoidable lot.
>
> *1b* culminating condition or end indicated as probable, inevitable, or having been reached.
>
> *2a* the predetermined course of events often conceived as a resistless power or agency: the foreordained future whether in general or of an individual.

Daniel H. Ludlow is professor emeritus of ancient scripture and former dean of Religious Education at Brigham Young University.

> *2b* continuing activity and functional behavior that tend to determine eventual status especially as to progress or decadence—usually used in plural.
>
> *3* a real or imaginary power or agency conceived as predetermining the course of events and choice of alternatives.

When I looked up the meaning of the root word *destiny,* I was surprised to note that it comes from the Latin and the French *"de + -stinare;* akin to *stare,* to stand" with the fundamental meaning of "to direct and impel inescapably on a fixed course." I say surprised for I remembered a similar experience some thirteen years ago when I was in Perth, Australia, and heard that the Brethren had announced that henceforth the Book of Mormon would have a subtitle: "Another Testament of Jesus Christ." I went to the national library in Perth to look up the word *testament.* There, in the largest dictionary of the English language that I could find, I noted that the word *testament* came into English from the Latin and the French from "a prehistoric Italic compound whose first and second constituents respectively are akin to Latin *tres* three and to Latin *stare* to stand."

I had never before associated the word *destiny* with the word *testament,* yet they both come from the same basic root, *stare,* meaning "to stand." By the time I had concluded pondering on the possible meanings of the word *destiny,* I realized I would need to do much more today than simply discuss the prophetic future of the house of Israel—a term many of us would associate with the word *destiny.* I would also need to include something of the historical past and of the present conditions associated with the house of Israel.

HOUSE OF ISRAEL

My attention then centered on the other major term in the title of this discussion: *house of Israel.* This time my sources were two:

The Exhaustive Concordance of the Bible, by James Strong, which, according to the subtitle, shows "every word of the text of the common English Version of the canonical books, and every occurrence of each word in regular order."[1] According to a reference in another book, "Dr. James Strong's *Exhaustive Concordance* of the King James translation was first issued in 1894 after a hundred men had worked on it for thirty years."[2]

An Exhaustive Concordance of the Book of Mormon, Doctrine and Covenants, and Pearl of Great Price, compiled by R. Gary Shapiro. The preface of this book indicates it "lists alphabetically all words exactly as they appear in the sacred text" with the additional note: "With the use of today's computer technology . . . the work was completed in four years."

I found that the term *house of Israel* appears 280 times in the scriptures. All the other major terms referring to the greater house of Israel are used only 70 times. (See the Appendix at the end of this chapter.)

TRUTH

Our review of some of the major scriptures and the teachings of the prophets in searching for truths concerning the house of Israel begins with the Book of Mormon. There we find this definition of *truth:*

> The Spirit speaketh the truth and lieth not. Wherefore, it speaketh of things as they really are, and of things as they really will be. [Jacob 4:13]

An even more complete definition is provided in the Doctrine and Covenants:

> And truth is knowledge of things as they are, and as they were, and as they are to come. [D&C 93:24]

Let us examine, then, some of the truths pertaining to the house of Israel, primarily those in the Bible and the Book of Mormon and those that have been clarified in the teachings of the Prophet Joseph Smith and of later prophets, seers, and revelators. In presenting these statements I am well aware of the admonition of Peter:

> Knowing this first, that no prophecy of the scripture is of any private interpretation. For the prophecy came not in old time by the will of man: but holy men of God spake as they were moved by the Holy Ghost. [2 Peter 1:20–21]

I am also aware that the Lord has declared in several places that in the mouth of two or three witnesses every word and truth shall be established:

> At the mouth of two witnesses, or at the mouth of three witnesses, shall the matter be established. [Deuteronomy 19:15]
>
> In the mouth of two or three witnesses shall every word be established. [2 Corinthians 13:1]
>
> Know ye not that the testimony of two nations is a witness unto you that I am God? [2 Nephi 29:8]
>
> In the mouth of two or three witnesses shall every word be established. [D&C 6:28]

In fact, the Lord declared that at least three scriptural witnesses would testify of his work:

> [Lord God of Hosts/Nephi] For behold, I shall speak unto the Jews and they shall write it; and I shall also speak unto the Nephites and they shall write it; and I shall also speak unto the other tribes of the house of Israel, which I have led away, and they shall write it; and I shall also speak unto all nations of the earth and they shall write it. . . .

> And it shall come to pass that my people, which are of the house of Israel, shall be gathered home unto the lands of their possessions; and my word also shall be gathered in one. And I will show unto them that fight against my word and against my people, who are of the house of Israel, that I am God, and that I covenanted with Abraham that I would remember his seed forever. [2 Nephi 29:12, 14]

THE TRUTHS OF THE HOUSE OF ISRAEL "AS THEY WERE" AND "AS THEY ARE"

We rely primarily on the teachings of the Old Testament concerning the origin and the early history of the house of Israel. The first time the word *Israel* appears in the Old Testament (and thus, I assume, the first time it is used upon the earth) is in connection with the man otherwise known as Jacob, the son of Isaac and the grandson of Abraham:

> [Angel/Jacob, son of Lehi] And he said, Thy name shall be called no more Jacob, but Israel: for as a prince hast thou power with God and with men, and hast prevailed. [Genesis 32:28]

> [God/Moses] And God said unto him, Thy name is Jacob: thy name shall not be called any more Jacob, but Israel shall be thy name: and he called his name Israel. [Genesis 35:10]

Thus, *Israel* becomes the family title of the family of Jacob. This family also becomes known collectively as the *house of Israel.* Because Jacob (or Israel) had twelve sons, his descendants are also known as the *twelve tribes of Israel* or simply as the *tribes of Israel* or as *Israelites.*

Usually the term *house of Israel* in the Old Testament can be read as though it were *family of Israel* or *descendants of Israel,* or even as *house of Jacob* or *descendants of Jacob.* For example, in Isaiah's writing, we see the term *house of Israel* used four times and the term *house of Jacob* used nine times, both terms clearly referring to the descendants of Jacob.

During the Old Testament period of the divided kingdom, the term *house of Israel* is used occasionally as though it were *kingdom of Israel,* usually in conjunction with the terms *house of Judah* or *kingdom of Judah.* Thus the Lord announces in Jeremiah 5:11, "The house of Israel and the house of Judah have dealt very treacherously against me," and in Jeremiah 11:10, "The house of Israel and the house of Judah have broken my covenant which I made with their fathers."

In the Book of Mormon, however, the term *house of Israel* is used consistently to refer to the *family* or to the *descendants* of Israel (Jacob). The term *house of Jacob* also appears fifteen times in the Book of Mormon, usually in reference to the descendants of Lehi as a "remnant" of the house of Jacob. The term *house of Judah* does not appear a single time in the Book of Mormon. This is consistent with the fact that the divided kingdom had ended in 722 B.C. with the capture of the kingdom of Israel by the Assyrians, some 122 years before the opening of the Book of Mormon.

The family designation for the descendants of Judah—*Jew*—is also used extensively in both the Bible and the Book of Mormon. It first appears as a plural (*Jews*) in the Bible in 2 Kings 16:6, Esther 2:5, and Jeremiah 34:9, and in the Book of Mormon in 1 Nephi 1:2. Together the words *Jew* and *Jews* appear 403 times in the scriptures: Old Testament, 92; New Testament, 197; Book of Mormon, 89; Doctrine and Covenants, 22; Pearl of Great Price, 3.

The faithful members of Lehi's descendants knew a great deal about the origin and early history of the house of Israel. In discussing the plates of brass obtained from Laban, Nephi notes that "they did contain the five books of Moses, which gave an account of the creation of the world, . . . and also a record of the Jews from the beginning, even down to the commencement of the reign of Zedekiah, king of Judah" (1 Nephi 5:11–12). Evidently by the time of Lehi, the meaning of the word *Jew* had been expanded to include those who were citizens of the kingdom of Judah as well as those who were literal descendants of Judah, the fourth son of Jacob.

> [Nephi, the son of Lehi] I have charity for the Jew—I say Jew, because I mean them from whence I came. [2 Nephi 33:8]

> [Nephi] And the things which shall be written out of the book shall be of great worth unto the children of men, and especially unto our seed, which is a remnant of the house of Israel. [2 Nephi 28:2]

It has been said, and it seems quite obvious, that a writer or speaker is usually much more effective in his presentation if he has a particular audience in mind as he prepares his material. This procedure should enable him to focus his materials more effectively. This I have tried to do in the preparation of this material. I sincerely believe that few, if any, groups on the face of the earth would know more about the destiny of the house of Israel than the Latter-day Saints.

It seems equally obvious that the audience could understand the message of the author or speaker more thoroughly if it knew something of the background of the person whose ideas are included in the presentation. Thus, to take advantage of this second principle, I have chosen to present materials on the destiny of the house of Israel that come from the background and experience of the Prophet Joseph Smith.

It is my firm conviction that at the time of the martyrdom of the Prophet Joseph Smith on 27 June 1844, he understood more about the destiny of the house of

Israel—including its origin, history, and prophesied future—than any person then living upon the earth, with the possible exceptions of translated beings, such as John the Beloved, the three Nephite disciples, and other "holy men" of God "that ye know not of" mentioned by the Lord in Doctrine and Covenants 49:8.

The remainder of this discussion consists primarily of the writings and teachings of the Prophet Joseph Smith concerning the destiny of the house of Israel as revealed in his visions and visitations of divine persons and messengers, in his translation of the Book of Mormon, in his inspired translation of the Bible, in revelations received on the subject, including those in the Doctrine and Covenants, in his revealing of truths in the books of Abraham and Moses in the Pearl of Great Price, and in other diverse and sundry manners.

Joseph Smith knew that the number of the house of Israel had been foreordained from before the foundations of the earth.

> [Paul] And hath made of one blood all nations of men for to dwell on all the face of the earth, and hath determined the times before appointed, and the bounds of their habitation. [Acts 17:26]
>
> [Moses] When the most High divided to the nations their inheritance, when he separated the sons of Adam, he set the bounds of the people according to the number of the children of Israel. [Deuteronomy 32:8]

Joseph Smith knew that God, who cannot and does not lie, has throughout the centuries made special promises to individuals and groups and nations of people, predicated on their obedience to certain laws and principles. These *covenants* are binding upon the Lord:

> [Lord] I, the Lord, am bound when ye do what I say; but when ye do not what I say, ye have no promise. [D&C 82:10]
>
> [Isaiah] The grass withereth, the flower fadeth: but the word of our God shall stand for ever. [Isaiah 40:8]

Joseph Smith knew that God had entered into sacred covenants with our father Abraham and that these promises had been reaffirmed through Isaac and through Jacob (Israel) and his descendants. Thus, the people of the house of Israel are a covenant people.

> [Lord/Moses] And the Lord said, Shall I hide from Abraham that thing which I do;
> Seeing that Abraham shall surely become a great and mighty nation, and all the nations of the earth shall be blessed in him? [Genesis 18:17–18]
>
> [Moses] For thou art an holy people unto the Lord thy God: the Lord thy God hath chosen thee to be a special people unto himself, above all people that are upon the face of the earth. [Deuteronomy 7:6]

Joseph Smith knew that God's covenant with ancient Israel, then living in the land of Israel, provided that they would remain in their promised lands so long as they were obedient to their part of the covenant. We read an example of these promises in Deuteronomy 28:1–14 (the blessings are identified individually for ease in comparing to the warnings listed later):

> And it shall come to pass, if thou shalt hearken diligently unto the voice of the Lord thy God, to observe and to do all his commandments . . . all these blessings shall come on thee, and overtake thee:
>
> [1.] The Lord thy God will set thee on high above all nations of the earth. [V. 1]
>
> [2.] Blessed shalt thou be in the city, and . . . in the field. [V. 3]

> [3.] Blessed shall be the fruit of thy body, and the fruit of thy ground, and the fruit of thy cattle. [V. 4]
>
> [4.] Blessed shall be thy basket and thy store. [V. 5]
>
> [5.] Blessed shalt thou be when thou comest in, and . . . goest out. [V. 6]
>
> [6.] The Lord shall cause thine enemies that rise up against thee to be smitten before thy face: they shall come out against thee one way, and flee before thee seven ways. [V. 7]
>
> [7.] The Lord shall command the blessing upon thee in thy storehouses, and in all that thou settest thine hand unto; . . . The Lord shall establish thee an holy people unto himself, . . . [and] shall make thee plenteous in goods, in the fruit of thy body, . . . thy cattle [and] thy ground. [Vv. 8–11]
>
> [8.] The Lord shall open unto thee his good treasure, the heaven to give the rain unto thy land, . . . and thou shalt lend unto many nations, and thou shalt not borrow. [V. 12]
>
> [9.] And the Lord shall make thee the head, and not the tail; and thou shalt be above only, and thou shalt not be beneath. [V. 13]
>
> [10.] And thou shalt not go aside from any of the words which I command thee this day, to the right hand, or to the left, to go after other gods to serve them. [V. 14]

Joseph Smith knew that when the people of the ancient house of Israel became disobedient to their promises, they (the kingdom of Israel) were taken into captivity by the Assyrians some 722 years before the prophesied birth of the Messiah, and the kingdom of Judah by the Babylonians in approximately 600 B.C. These dispersions and other calamities came upon them because of their disobedience, as recorded in Deuteronomy 28:15–67 (the warnings here are identified individually for ease in comparing to the blessings listed above):

> But it shall come to pass, if thou wilt not hearken unto the voice of the Lord thy God, to observe to do all his commandments and his statutes . . . that all these curses shall come upon thee, and overtake thee. [V. 15]
>
> [1.] Thy sons and thy daughters shall be given unto another people, and thine eyes shall look, and fail with longing for them all the day long: and there shall be no might in thine hand. The fruit of thy land, and all thy labours, shall a nation which thou knowest not eat up; and thou shalt be only oppressed and crushed. . . . The Lord shall bring thee, and thy king which thou shalt set over thee, unto a nation which neither thou nor thy fathers have known; and there shalt thou serve other gods, wood and stone. And thou shalt become an astonishment, a proverb, and a byword, among all nations whither the Lord shall lead thee. . . . Thou shalt beget sons and daughters, but . . . they shall go into captivity. . . . And ye shall be left few in number, whereas ye were as the stars of heaven for multitude; because thou wouldest not obey the voice of the Lord thy God. . . . And the Lord shall scatter thee among all people, from the one end of the earth even unto the other. . . . And among these nations shalt thou find no ease, neither shall the sole of thy foot have rest: but the Lord shall give thee there a trembling heart, and failing of eyes, and sorrow of mind: And thy life shall hang in doubt before thee; and thou shalt fear day and night, and shalt have none assurance of thy life: In the morning thou shalt say, Would God it were even! and at even thou shalt say, Would God it were morning! for the fear of thine heart wherewith thou shalt fear, and for the sight of thine eyes which thou shalt see. [Vv. 32–33, 36–37, 41, 62, 64–67]

[2.] Cursed shalt thou be in the city, and . . . in the field. [V. 16]

[3.] Cursed shall be the fruit of thy body [and] land [and] flocks. [V. 18]

[4.] Cursed shall be thy basket and thy store. [V. 17]

[5.] Cursed shalt thou be when thou comest in, and . . . goest out. [V. 19]

[6.] The Lord shall cause thee to be smitten before thine enemies: thou shalt go out one way against them, and flee seven ways before them. [V. 25]

[7.] The Lord shall send upon thee cursing, vexation, and rebuke, in all that thou settest thine hand . . . to do. [V. 20]

[8.] The Lord shall smite thee with a consumption, and with a fever, and with an inflammation, and with an extreme burning, and with the sword, and with blasting, and with mildew; and they shall pursue thee until thou perish. And thy heaven that is over thy head shall be brass, and the earth that is under thee shall be iron. The Lord shall make the rain of thy land powder and dust: from heaven shall it come down upon thee, until thou be destroyed. [Vv. 22–24]

[9.] And thou shalt grope at noonday, as the blind gropeth in darkness, and thou shalt not prosper in thy ways: and thou shalt be only oppressed and spoiled evermore, and no man shall save thee. [V. 29]

[10.] The Lord shall bring thee . . . unto a nation . . . and there shalt thou serve other gods, wood and stone. [V. 36]

And the Lord shall scatter thee . . . and there thou shalt serve other gods, . . . even wood and stone. [V. 64]

Joseph Smith knew that the house of Israel was likened to an olive tree, as explained in the allegory of Zenos in Jacob 5, and that many branches of the house of Israel were scattered throughout the earth, even to the nethermost parts of the vineyard:

> [Nephi, son of Lehi] Yea, even my father spake . . . concerning the house of Israel, that they should be compared like unto an olive-tree, whose branches should be broken off and should be scattered upon all the face of the earth. [1 Nephi 10:12]

> [Lord] For behold, thus saith the Lord, I will liken thee, O house of Israel, like unto a tame olive-tree, which a man took and nourished in his vineyard; and it grew, and waxed old, and began to decay. [Jacob 5:3]

Joseph Smith knew that when another large group of the house of Israel (then known as the kingdom of Judah) was disobedient, they would be taken into captivity by the Babylonians but that after a time they would be allowed to return to their promised lands of inheritance in the land of Israel before the Messiah appeared to them.

> [Chronicler] Now in the first year of Cyrus king of Persia, that the word of the Lord spoken by the mouth of Jeremiah might be accomplished, the Lord stirred up the spirit of Cyrus king of Persia, that he made a proclamation throughout all his kingdom, and put it also in writing, saying,
>
> Thus saith Cyrus king of Persia, All the kingdoms of the earth hath the Lord God of heaven given me; and he hath charged me to build him an house in Jerusalem, which is in Judah. Who is there among you of all his people? The Lord his God be with him, and let him go up. [2 Chronicles 36:22–23; compare Ezra 1:1–3]

> [Ezra] Now in the first year of Cyrus king of Persia, that the word of the Lord by the mouth of Jeremiah might be fulfilled, the Lord stirred up the spirit of Cyrus king of Persia, that he made a proclamation throughout all his kingdom, and put it also in writing,

> saying,
>
> Thus saith Cyrus king of Persia, The Lord God of heaven hath given me all the kingdoms of the earth; and he hath charged me to build him an house at Jerusalem, which is in Judah.
>
> Who is there among you of all his people? his God be with him, and let him go up to Jerusalem, which is in Judah, and build the house of the Lord God of Israel, (he is the God,) which is in Jerusalem.
>
> And whosoever remaineth in any place where he sojourneth, let the men of his place help him with silver, and with gold, and with goods, and with beasts, beside the freewill offering for the house of God that is in Jerusalem.
>
> Then rose up the chief of the fathers of Judah and Benjamin, and the priests, and the Levites, with all them whose spirit God had raised, to go up to build the house of the Lord which is in Jerusalem.
>
> And all they that were about them strengthened their hands with vessels of silver, with gold, with goods, and with beasts, and with precious things, beside all that was willingly offered. [Ezra 1:1–6; compare 2 Chronicles 36:22–23]

> [Ezra] Now these are the children of the province that went up out of the captivity, of those which had been carried away, whom Nebuchadnezzar the king of Babylon had carried away unto Babylon, and came again unto Jerusalem and Judah, every one unto his city. [Ezra 2:1]

Joseph Smith knew that a large branch of the house of Israel that was scattered was made up of the descendants of Lehi, Zoram, Ishmael, Zarahemla, and Mulek, who were led to their promised lands of inheritance in the lands of the everlasting hills shaped as the great wings of a bird, even the lands of North and South America.

> [Jacob to Joseph] The blessings of thy father have

> prevailed above the blessings of my progenitors unto the utmost bound of the everlasting hills: they shall be on the head of Joseph, and on the crown of the head of him that was separate from his brethren. [Genesis 49:26]

> [Isaiah] Woe to the land shadowing with wings, which is beyond the rivers of Ethiopia: . . .
>
> All ye inhabitants of the world, and dwellers on the earth, see ye, when he lifteth up an ensign on the mountains; and when he bloweth a trumpet, hear ye. [Isaiah 18:1, 3]

Joseph Smith knew that the descendants of Lehi in the Book of Mormon were descendants of Jacob (Israel) through the loins of Joseph.

> [Nephi, son of Lehi] My father, Lehi, . . . found upon the plates of brass a genealogy of his fathers; wherefore he knew that he was a descendant of Joseph; yea, even that Joseph who was the son of Jacob, who was sold into Egypt. [1 Nephi 5:14]

> [Nephi, son of Lehi, to his brethren] Behold, I say unto you, that the house of Israel was compared unto an olive-tree, by the Spirit of the Lord which was in our father; and behold are we not broken off from the house of Israel, and are we not a branch of the house of Israel? [1 Nephi 15:12]

> [Jacob, son of Lehi] And now, the words which I shall read are they which Isaiah spake concerning all the house of Israel; wherefore, they may be likened unto you, for ye are of the house of Israel. And there are many things which have been spoken by Isaiah which may be likened unto you, because ye are of the house of Israel. [2 Nephi 6:5]

Joseph Smith knew that the scriptures—both the Bible and the Book of Mormon—contained many of the covenants the Lord had made with the house of Israel.

> [Lord/Ezekiel] Moreover, thou son of man, take thee one stick, and write upon it, For Judah, and for the children of Israel his companions: then take another stick, and write upon it, For Joseph, the stick of Ephraim, and for all the house of Israel his companions. [Ezekiel 37:16]

> [Nephi, son of Lehi] For the fulness of mine intent is that I may persuade men to come unto the God of Abraham, and the God of Isaac, and the God of Jacob, and be saved. [1 Nephi 6:4]

> [Angel to Nephi, son of Lehi] And he said: Behold it proceedeth out of the mouth of a Jew. And I, Nephi, beheld it; and he said unto me: The book that thou beholdest is a record of the Jews, which contains the covenants of the Lord, which he hath made unto the house of Israel; and it also containeth many of the prophecies of the holy prophets; and it is a record like unto the engravings which are upon the plates of brass, save there are not so many; nevertheless, they contain the covenants of the Lord, which he hath made unto the house of Israel. [1 Nephi 13:23]

> [Mormon] And behold, they shall go unto the unbelieving of the Jews; and for this intent shall they go—that they may be persuaded that Jesus is the Christ, the Son of the living God; that the Father may bring about, through his most Beloved, his great and eternal purpose, in restoring the Jews, or all the house of Israel, to the land of their inheritance, which the Lord their God hath given them, unto the fulfilling of his covenant. [Mormon 5:14]

Joseph Smith knew that the law of Moses was given to the house of Israel in ancient times to prepare them for the coming of Jesus Christ.

> [Nephi, son of Lehi] Behold, my soul delighteth in proving unto my people the truth of the coming of

> Christ; for, for this end hath the law of Moses been given; and all things which have been given of God from the beginning of the world, unto man, are the typifying of him. [2 Nephi 11:4]
>
> [Nephi, son of Lehi] And, notwithstanding we believe in Christ, we keep the law of Moses, and look forward with steadfastness unto Christ, until the law shall be fulfilled.
>
> For, for this end was the law given; wherefore the law hath become dead unto us, and we are made alive in Christ because of our faith; yet we keep the law because of the commandments.
>
> And we talk of Christ, we rejoice in Christ, we preach of Christ, we prophesy of Christ, and we write according to our prophecies, that our children may know to what source they may look for a remission of their sins. [2 Nephi 25:24–26]

Joseph Smith knew that a main purpose of the writing and the coming forth of the Book of Mormon was to convince the Gentiles and the house of Israel that Jesus Christ is the Son of God. On the title page of the Book of Mormon we read:

> [Moroni] It is an abridgment of the record of the people of Nephi, and also of the Lamanites—Written to the Lamanites, who are a remnant of the house of Israel; and also to Jew and Gentile—Written by way of commandment, and also by the spirit of prophecy and of revelation—. . . Which is to show unto the remnant of the house of Israel what great things the Lord hath done for their fathers; and that they may know the covenants of the Lord, that they are not cast off forever—And also to the convincing of the Jew and Gentile that Jesus is the Christ, the Eternal God, manifesting himself unto all nations.

We read further:

> [Nephi, son of Lehi] And now, my beloved brethren, and also Jew, and all ye ends of the earth, hearken unto these words and believe in Christ; and if ye believe not in these words believe in Christ. And if ye shall believe in Christ ye will believe in these words, for they are the words of Christ, and he hath given them unto me. [2 Nephi 33:10]

Joseph Smith knew that the God who made these promises to ancient covenant Israel is Jehovah, who came to earth as the promised Messiah (note particularly JST Exodus 6:3).

> [Lord/Moses] And I appeared unto Abraham, unto Isaac, and unto Jacob, by the name of God Almighty, but by my name Jehovah was I not known to them. [Exodus 6:3]
>
> [Lord/Moses] And I appeared unto Abraham, unto Isaac, and unto Jacob. I am the Lord God Almighty; the Lord Jehovah. And was not my name known unto them? [JST Exodus 6:3]
>
> [Psalmist] That men may know that thou, whose name alone is Jehovah, art the most high over all the earth. [Psalm 83:18]
>
> [Isaiah] Behold, God is my salvation; I will trust, and not be afraid: for the Lord Jehovah is my strength and my song; he also is become my salvation. [Isaiah 12:2]
>
> [Isaiah] Trust ye in the Lord for ever: for in the Lord Jehovah is everlasting strength. [Isaiah 26:4]

Joseph Smith knew that some members of the house of Israel anciently knew that Jehovah in the Old Testament was the Messiah and the same personage who later became known by the name-title of Jesus Christ in the New Testament. Even many years before the birth of the Messiah upon the earth, favored groups within the house of Israel knew—

1. That the angel Gabriel would announce the coming birth of the Messiah to a virgin living in Nazareth who was the foreordained mother of the Son of God, even a virgin who was fairer than any other virgin. Nephi wrote that in his vision "I beheld the city of Nazareth; and in the city of Nazareth I beheld a virgin . . . most beautiful and fair above all other virgins," and the angel declared to Nephi, "The virgin whom thou seest is the mother of the Son of God, after the manner of the flesh" (1 Nephi 11:13, 15, 18).

2. That the name of the Messiah's mother would be Mary (Mosiah 3:8; Alma 7:10).

3. That he would be born in Bethlehem in the inheritance of Judah (Micah 5:2).

4. That a new star would announce his birth (Helaman 14:5; 3 Nephi 1:21).

5. That the Messiah would be born six hundred years after the beginning of the reign of Zedekiah, king of Judah. Thus, Nephi wrote that his father left Jerusalem "in the . . . first year of the reign of Zedekiah, king of Judah" (1 Nephi 1:4) and "even six hundred years from the time that my father left Jerusalem, a prophet would the Lord God raise up among the Jews—even a Messiah, or, in other words, a Savior of the world . . . or this Redeemer of the world" (1 Nephi 10:4–5). In 2 Nephi 25:19 he adds the confirming witness: "For according to the words of the prophets, the Messiah cometh in six hundred years from the time that my father left Jerusalem; and according to the words of the prophets, and also the word of the angel of God, his name shall be Jesus Christ, the Son of God." Nephi also testified: "The Son of God was the Messiah who should come" (1 Nephi 10:17).

6. That he would come forth out of Egypt (Hosea 11:1) to dwell in the inheritance lands of Zebulon and

Naphtali (Isaiah 9:1–2), where those who were sitting in darkness would see a great light.

7. That he would make a triumphal entry into Jerusalem seated on the foal of an ass (Jeremiah 9:9; Matthew 21:6–11).

8. That his name-titles would include Jesus Christ (Matthew 16:16), the Messiah (1 Nephi 10:4), Immanuel (Isaiah 7:14), the Son of the Highest (Luke 1:32), the Son of Man of Holiness (Moses 6:57), the Son of David (Isaiah 11:1, 10), the Only Begotten of the Father in the flesh (2 Nephi 25:12), the Lamb of God who is the son of the Eternal Father (1 Nephi 11:21), the Messenger of the Covenant (Malachi 3:1), the Savior and Redeemer of mankind (Mormon 3:14; Isaiah 41:14), "Wonderful, Counsellor, The mighty God, The everlasting Father, The Prince of Peace" (Isaiah 9:6).

9. That at the time of his death a special sign should be given to those of the house of Israel, yea, "three days of darkness . . . should be a sign given of his death unto those who should inhabit the isles of the sea, more especially given unto those who are of the house of Israel" (1 Nephi 19:10). Then, continued the prophet Zenos, "As for those who are at Jerusalem, . . . they shall be scourged by all people, because they crucify the God of Israel, and turn their hearts aside, rejecting signs and wonders, and the power and glory of the God of Israel. And because they turn their hearts aside, . . . and have despised the Holy One of Israel, they shall wander in the flesh, and perish, and become a hiss and a byword, and be hated among all nations" (1 Nephi 19:13–14).

Joseph Smith knew that despite all these prophecies, the Jews—a large proportion of the house of Israel among whom the Messiah lived—had rejected Jesus Christ and their leaders agreed to his death. As Jacob the son of Lehi prophesied hundreds of years before the birth of the Messiah, the Jews would be a "stiffnecked people" who would despise "the words of plainness" and would seek "for things that they could not understand. Wherefore, because of their blindness, which blindness came by looking beyond the mark," they would "reject the stone upon which they might build and have safe foundation" (Jacob 4:14–15). Jacob also revealed that the Messiah would be born among the Jews, because it was needful that his life should be taken and no other people would take the life of their Creator:

> [Jacob, son of Lehi] It must needs be expedient that Christ—for in the last night the angel spake unto me that this should be his name—should come among the Jews, among those who are of the more wicked part of the world; and they shall crucify him—for thus it behooveth our God, and there is none other nation on earth that would crucify their God. [2 Nephi 10:3]

Joseph Smith knew that when the Messiah came to the earth, he lived in the lands of his ancestors among his kindred "friends" but that he was rejected of them and even crucified in their midst.

> [Nephi, son of Lehi] When the day cometh that the Only Begotten of the Father, yea, even the Father of heaven and of earth, shall manifest himself unto them in the flesh, behold, they will reject him, because of their iniquities, and the hardness of their hearts, and the stiffness of their necks. [2 Nephi 25:12]

> [Jacob, son of Lehi] Nevertheless, the Lord has shown unto me that they should return again. And he also has shown unto me that the Lord God, the Holy One of Israel, should manifest himself unto them in the flesh; and after he should manifest himself they should scourge him and crucify him, according to the words of the angel who spake it unto me. [2 Nephi 6:9]

> [King Benjamin] And lo, he cometh unto his own, that salvation might come unto the children of men even through faith on his name; and even after all this they shall consider him a man, and say that he hath a devil, and shall scourge him, and shall crucify him. [Mosiah 3:9]

Joseph Smith knew that after Jesus Christ was resurrected from the dead, he appeared not only to representatives of the Jews in the land of Israel but also to other branches of the house of Israel, including those in the Americas and even to the lost tribes of Israel. Thus, we read these words of the resurrected Jesus Christ to the righteous Lehites who survived the destructions associated with his crucifixion:

> [Jesus Christ] And verily I say unto you, that ye are they of whom I said: Other sheep I have which are not of this fold; them also I must bring, and they shall hear my voice; and there shall be one fold, and one shepherd.
>
> But behold, ye have both heard my voice, and seen me; and ye are my sheep, and ye are numbered among those whom the Father hath given me. [3 Nephi 15:21, 24]

> [Jesus Christ] And verily, verily, I say unto you that I have other sheep, which are not of this land, neither of the land of Jerusalem, neither in any parts of that land round about whither I have been to minister.
>
> For they of whom I speak are they who have not as yet heard my voice; neither have I at any time manifested myself unto them.
>
> But I have received a commandment of the Father that I shall go unto them, and that they shall hear my voice, and shall be numbered among my sheep, that there may be one fold and one shepherd; therefore I go to show myself unto them. [3 Nephi 16:1–3]

> [Jesus Christ] But now I go unto the Father, and also

to show myself unto the lost tribes of Israel, for they are not lost unto the Father, for he knoweth whither he hath taken them. [3 Nephi 17:4]

Joseph Smith knew that as a result of their rejection of Jesus Christ and their subsequent disobedience and rebellion, the descendants of the kingdom of Judah (one part of the house of Israel), then known as Jews, were separated again from the lands of their inheritance and sifted like corn among the nations of the earth. This scattering was accomplished by the Romans in the first century after the birth of the Messiah.

[Jacob, son of Lehi] For behold, the Lord has shown me that those who were at Jerusalem, from whence we came, have been slain and carried away captive. [2 Nephi 6:8]

[Jacob, son of Lehi] But because of priestcrafts and iniquities, they at Jerusalem will stiffen their necks against him, that he be crucified.

Wherefore, because of their iniquities, destructions, famines, pestilences, and bloodshed shall come upon them; and they who shall not be destroyed shall be scattered among all nations. [2 Nephi 10:5–6]

[Nephi, son of Lehi] And behold it shall come to pass that after the Messiah hath risen from the dead, and hath manifested himself unto his people, unto as many as will believe on his name, behold, Jerusalem shall be destroyed again; for wo unto them that fight against God and the people of his church.

Wherefore, the Jews shall be scattered among all nations; yea, and also Babylon shall be destroyed; wherefore, the Jews shall be scattered by other nations. [2 Nephi 25:14–15]

[Lord/Amos] For, lo, I will command, and I will sift the house of Israel among all nations, like as corn is sifted in a sieve, yet shall not the least grain fall upon the earth. [Amos 9:9]

> [Nephi, son of Lehi] And again: Hearken, O ye house of Israel, all ye that are broken off and are driven out because of the wickedness of the pastors of my people; yea, all ye that are broken off, that are scattered abroad, who are of my people, O house of Israel. Listen, O isles, unto me, and hearken ye people from far. [1 Nephi 21:1; compare Isaiah 49:1]

> [Nephi, son of Lehi] Wherefore, the things of which I have read are things pertaining to things both temporal and spiritual; for it appears that the house of Israel, sooner or later, will be scattered upon all the face of the earth, and also among all nations. [1 Nephi 22:3]

Joseph Smith knew that after the Savior's appearances in the meridian of time, there was an apostasy from the covenants of God by the chosen people, a period of darkness of spiritual truths upon the earth that was recognized later by many as the "dark ages," when the heavens were even as brass.

> [Lord/Amos] Behold, the days come, saith the Lord God, that I will send a famine in the land, not a famine of bread, nor a thirst for water, but of hearing the words of the Lord:
>
> And they shall wander from sea to sea, and from the north even to the east, they shall run to and fro to seek the word of the Lord, and shall not find it. [Amos 8:11–12]

> [Lord/Micah] Thus saith the Lord. . . .
>
> Therefore night shall be unto you, that ye shall not have a vision; and it shall be dark unto you, that ye shall not divine; and the sun shall go down over the prophets, and the day shall be dark over them.
>
> Then shall the seers be ashamed, and the diviners confounded: yea, they shall all cover their lips; for there is no answer of God. [Micah 3:5–7]

> [Paul] For the time will come when they will not

> endure sound doctrine; but after their own lusts shall they heap to themselves teachers, having itching ears;
> And they shall turn away their ears from the truth, and shall be turned unto fables. [2 Timothy 4:3–4]

Joseph Smith knew, for the prophets of the Old Testament and the apostles of the New Testament had so declared, that a time of restitution, or restoration, would occur, when the iron ceiling of heaven would be shattered and the rock of revelation coming directly from the Rock of Israel would again return to the earth.

> [Peter] And he shall send Jesus Christ, which before was preached unto you:
> Whom the heaven must receive until the times of restitution of all things, which God hath spoken by the mouth of all his holy prophets since the world began. [Acts 3:20–21]

> [Paul] Having made known unto us the mystery of his will, according to his good pleasure which he hath purposed in himself:
> That in the dispensation of the fulness of times he might gather together in one all things in Christ, both which are in heaven, and which are on earth; even in him. [Ephesians 1:9–10]

> [Lord/Isaiah] Wherefore the Lord said, Forasmuch as this people draw near me with their mouth, and with their lips do honour me, but have removed their heart far from me, and their fear toward me is taught by the precept of men:
> Therefore, behold, I will proceed to do a marvellous work among this people, even a marvellous work and a wonder: for the wisdom of their wise men shall perish, and the understanding of their prudent men shall be hid. [Isaiah 29:13–14]

Joseph Smith knew that as part of this restoration, or restitution, in the latter days, the covenants of the Lord would once again be made available to the scattered segments of the house of Israel.

> [Nephi, son of Lehi] Wherefore, our father hath not spoken of our seed alone, but also of all the house of Israel, pointing to the covenant which should be fulfilled in the latter days; which covenant the Lord made to our father Abraham, saying: In thy seed shall all the kindreds of the earth be blessed. [1 Nephi 15:18]

> [Nephi, son of Lehi] Wherefore, the Lord God will proceed to make bare his arm in the eyes of all the nations, in bringing about his covenants and his gospel unto those who are of the house of Israel.
>
> Wherefore, he will bring them again out of captivity, and they shall be gathered together to the lands of their inheritance; and they shall be brought out of obscurity and out of darkness; and they shall know that the Lord is their Savior and their Redeemer, the Mighty One of Israel. [1 Nephi 22:11–12]

> [Lord God of Hosts/Nephi] But behold, there shall be many—at that day when I shall proceed to do a marvelous work among them, that I may remember my covenants which I have made unto the children of men, that I may set my hand again the second time to recover my people, which are of the house of Israel;
>
> And also, that I may remember the promises which I have made unto thee, Nephi, and also unto thy father, that I would remember your seed; and that the words of your seed should proceed forth out of my mouth unto your seed; and my words shall hiss forth unto the ends of the earth, for a standard unto my people, which are of the house of Israel. [2 Nephi 29:1–2]

> [Mormon] And as surely as the Lord liveth, will he gather in from the four quarters of the earth all the remnant of the seed of Jacob, who are scattered abroad upon all the face of the earth.

> And as he hath covenanted with all the house of Jacob, even so shall the covenant wherewith he hath covenanted with the house of Jacob be fulfilled in his own due time, unto the restoring all the house of Jacob unto the knowledge of the covenant that he hath covenanted with them.
>
> And then shall they know their Redeemer, who is Jesus Christ, the Son of God; and then shall they be gathered in from the four quarters of the earth unto their own lands, from whence they have been dispersed; yea, as the Lord liveth so shall it be. Amen. [3 Nephi 5:24–26]

Joseph Smith knew that in the last days some of the descendants of Lehi, known as a remnant of the Jews, would accept the gospel and become part of covenant Israel once again.

> [Lehi] Wherefore, Joseph truly saw our day. And he obtained a promise of the Lord, that out of the fruit of his loins the Lord God would raise up a righteous branch unto the house of Israel; not the Messiah, but a branch which was to be broken off, nevertheless, to be remembered in the covenants of the Lord that the Messiah should be made manifest unto them in the latter days, in the spirit of power, unto the bringing of them out of darkness unto light—yea, out of hidden darkness and out of captivity unto freedom. [2 Nephi 3:5]

> [Jacob, son of Lehi] And behold how great the covenants of the Lord, and how great his condescensions unto the children of men; and because of his greatness, and his grace and mercy, he has promised unto us that our seed shall not utterly be destroyed, according to the flesh, but that he would preserve them; and in future generations they shall become a righteous branch unto the house of Israel. [2 Nephi 9:53]

> [Nephi, son of Lehi] And after the house of Israel

should be scattered they should be gathered together again; or, in fine, after the Gentiles had received the fulness of the Gospel, the natural branches of the olive-tree, or the remnants of the house of Israel, should be grafted in, or come to the knowledge of the true Messiah, their Lord and their Redeemer. [1 Nephi 10:14]

[Nephi, son of Lehi] And at that day shall the remnant of our seed know that they are of the house of Israel, and that they are the covenant people of the Lord; and then shall they know and come to the knowledge of their forefathers, and also to the knowledge of the gospel of their Redeemer, which was ministered unto their fathers by him; wherefore, they shall come to the knowledge of their Redeemer and the very points of his doctrine, that they may know how to come unto him and be saved. . . .

Yea; they shall be remembered again among the house of Israel; they shall be grafted in, being a natural branch of the olive-tree, into the true olive-tree. [1 Nephi 15:14, 16]

[Jacob, son of Lehi] For behold, the Lord God has led away from time to time from the house of Israel, according to his will and pleasure. And now behold, the Lord remembereth all them who have been broken off, wherefore he remembereth us also. [2 Nephi 10:22]

[Jesus Christ] For it is wisdom in the Father that they should be established in this land, and be set up as a free people by the power of the Father, that these things might come forth from them unto a remnant of your seed, that the covenant of the Father may be fulfilled which he hath covenanted with his people, O house of Israel. [3 Nephi 21:4]

[Mormon] But behold, it shall come to pass that they shall be driven and scattered by the Gentiles; and after they have been driven and scattered by the

Gentiles, behold, then will the Lord remember the covenant which he made unto Abraham and unto all the house of Israel. [Mormon 5:20]

Joseph Smith knew that after many generations the part of the house of Israel known as the house of Judah, or the Jews, would return a second time to the lands of their inheritance.

[Nephi, son of Lehi] And after they have been scattered, and the Lord God hath scourged them by other nations for the space of many generations, yea, even down from generation to generation until they shall be persuaded to believe in Christ, the Son of God, and the atonement, which is infinite for all mankind—and when that day shall come that they shall believe in Christ, and worship the Father in his name, with pure hearts and clean hands, and look not forward any more for another Messiah, then, at that time, the day will come that it must needs be expedient that they should believe these things. [2 Nephi 25:16]

[Nephi, son of Lehi] Yea, then will he remember the isles of the sea; yea, and all the people who are of the house of Israel, will I gather in, saith the Lord, according to the words of the prophet Zenos, from the four quarters of the earth. [1 Nephi 19:16]

[Jacob, son of Lehi] And now, my beloved brethren, I have read these things [Isaiah 50–52:2] that ye might know concerning the covenants of the Lord that he has covenanted with all the house of Israel—

That he has spoken unto the Jews by the mouth of his holy prophets, even from the beginning down, from generation to generation, until the time comes that they shall be restored to the true church and fold of God; when they shall be gathered home to the lands of their inheritance, and shall be established in all their lands of promise. [2 Nephi 9:1–2]

[Jacob, son of Lehi] But behold, thus saith the Lord

God: When the day cometh that they [descendants of those at Jerusalem at the time of the crucifixion] shall believe in me, that I am Christ, then have I covenanted with their fathers that they shall be restored in the flesh, upon the earth, unto the lands of their inheritance.

And it shall come to pass that they shall be gathered in from their long dispersion, from the isles of the sea, and from the four parts of the earth; and the nations of the Gentiles shall be great in the eyes of me, saith God, in carrying them forth to the lands of their inheritance. [2 Nephi 10:7–8]

[Lord/Jeremiah] In those days the house of Judah shall walk with the house of Israel, and they shall come together out of the land of the north to the land that I have given for an inheritance unto your fathers. [Jeremiah 3:18]

[Lord/Jeremiah] Therefore, behold, the days come, saith the Lord, that they shall no more say, The Lord liveth, which brought up the children of Israel out of the land of Egypt;

But, The Lord liveth, which brought up and which led the seed of the house of Israel out of the north country, and from all countries whither I had driven them; and they shall dwell in their own land. [Jeremiah 23:7–8]

[Isaiah] And he shall set up an ensign for the nations, and shall assemble the outcasts of Israel, and gather together the dispersed of Judah from the four corners of the earth. [Isaiah 11:12]

[Joseph Smith] He [Moroni] quoted the eleventh chapter of Isaiah, saying that it was about to be fulfilled. [Joseph Smith–History 1:40]

[Lord God/Ezekiel] Thus saith the Lord God; When I shall have gathered the house of Israel from the people among whom they are scattered, and shall be sanctified in them in the sight of the heathen, then shall they dwell in their land that I have given to my servant Jacob. [Ezekiel 28:25]

[Lord God/Ezekiel] And I will multiply men upon you, all the house of Israel, even all of it: and the cities shall be inhabited, and the wastes shall be builded. [Ezekiel 36:10]

[Lord/Zechariah] And many nations shall be joined to the Lord in that day, and shall be my people: and I will dwell in the midst of thee, and thou shalt know that the Lord of hosts hath sent me unto thee.

And the Lord shall inherit Judah his portion in the holy land, and shall choose Jerusalem again. [Zechariah 2:11–12]

Joseph Smith knew that at the time of the second return of the Jews to their promised land, powers and forces on the earth would seek their destruction and try to prevent their returning to their promised land. Nevertheless, the Lord would preserve them as a people and enable them to reclaim their lands.

[Jacob, son of Lehi] The Messiah will set himself again the second time to recover them [the Jews]; wherefore, he will manifest himself unto them in power and great glory, unto the destruction of their enemies. [2 Nephi 6:14]

[Nephi, son of Lehi] And every nation which shall war against thee, O house of Israel, shall be turned one against another, and they shall fall into the pit which they digged to ensnare the people of the Lord. And all that fight against Zion shall be destroyed. [1 Nephi 22:14]

[Nephi, son of Lehi] For the Lord will have mercy on Jacob, and will yet choose Israel, and set them in their own land; and the strangers shall be joined with them, and they shall cleave to the house of Jacob.

And the people shall take them and bring them to their place; yea, from far unto the ends of the earth;

and they shall return to their lands of promise. And the house of Israel shall possess them . . . and they shall take them captives unto whom they were captives; and they shall rule over their oppressors. [2 Nephi 24:1–2; compare Isaiah 14:1–2]

[Isaiah] For the Lord will have mercy on Jacob, and will yet choose Israel, and set them in their own land: and the strangers shall be joined with them, and they shall cleave to the house of Jacob.

And the people shall take them, and bring them to their place: and the house of Israel shall possess them in the land of the Lord for servants and handmaids: and they shall take them captives, whose captives they were; and they shall rule over their oppressors. [Isaiah 14:1–2; compare 2 Nephi 24:1–2]

[Lord/Isaiah/Lord] Behold, they shall surely gather together against thee, not by me; whosoever shall gather together against thee shall fall for thy sake. . . . No weapon that is formed against thee shall prosper. [3 Nephi 22:15, 17]

[Lord/Zechariah] Behold, I will make Jerusalem a cup of trembling unto all the people round about, when they shall be in the siege both against Judah and against Jerusalem. . . .

And in that day will I make Jerusalem a burdensome stone for all people: all that burden themselves with it shall be cut in pieces, though all the people of the earth be gathered together against it.

In that day will I make the governors of Judah like an hearth of fire among the wood, and like a torch of fire in a sheaf; and they shall devour all the people round about, on the right hand and on the left: and Jerusalem shall be inhabited again in her own place, even in Jerusalem.

The Lord also shall save the tents of Judah first, that the glory of the house of David and the glory of the

> inhabitants of Jerusalem do not magnify themselves against Judah.
>
> In that day shall the Lord defend the inhabitants of Jerusalem; and he that is feeble among them at that day shall be as David; and the house of David shall be as God, as the angel of the Lord before them.
>
> And it shall come to pass in that day, that I will seek to destroy all the nations that come against Jerusalem. [Zechariah 12:2–3, 6–9]

Joseph Smith knew that although the Jews had rejected the covenants of the gospel at the first coming of the Messiah, yet in the last days they would have another chance to become a covenant people of the Lord, together with other branches of the house of Israel.

> [Nephi, son of Lehi] I spake unto them concerning the restoration of the Jews in the latter days. And I did rehearse unto them the words of Isaiah, who spake concerning the restoration of the Jews, or of the house of Israel. [1 Nephi 15:19–20]

> [Lord/Jacob, son of Lehi] But behold, thus saith the Lord God: When the day cometh that they shall believe in me, that I am Christ, then have I covenanted with their fathers that they shall be restored in the flesh, upon the earth, unto the lands of their inheritance. [2 Nephi 10:7]

> [Jacob, son of Lehi] And how merciful is our God unto us, for he remembereth the house of Israel, both roots and branches; and he stretches forth his hands unto them all the day long; and they are a stiffnecked and a gainsaying people; but as many as will not harden their hearts shall be saved in the kingdom of God. [Jacob 6:4]

> [Jesus Christ] And then will I gather them in from the four quarters of the earth; and then will I fulfill the covenant which the Father hath made unto all the people of the house of Israel. [3 Nephi 16:5]

[Jesus Christ] And when these things come to pass that thy seed shall begin to know these things—it shall be a sign unto them, that they may know that the work of the Father hath already commenced unto the fulfilling of the covenant which he hath made unto the people who are of the house of Israel. [3 Nephi 21:7]

[Moroni] And ye need not imagine in your hearts that the words which have been spoken are vain, for behold, the Lord will remember his covenant which he hath made unto his people of the house of Israel. . . .

Yea, and ye need not any longer hiss, nor spurn, nor make game of the Jews, nor any of the remnant of the house of Israel; for behold, the Lord remembereth his covenant unto them, and he will do unto them according to that which he hath sworn.

Therefore ye need not suppose that ye can turn the right hand of the Lord unto the left, that he may not execute judgment unto the fulfilling of the covenant which he hath made unto the house of Israel. [3 Nephi 29:3, 8–9]

[Moroni] And awake, and arise from the dust, O Jerusalem; yea, and put on thy beautiful garments, O daughter of Zion; and strengthen thy stakes and enlarge thy borders forever, that thou mayest no more be confounded, that the covenants of the Eternal Father which he hath made unto thee, O house of Israel, may be fulfilled. [Moroni 10:31]

[Lord/Jeremiah] At the same time, saith the Lord, will I be the God of all the families of Israel, and they shall be my people. . . .

Behold, the days come, saith the Lord, that I will make a new covenant with the house of Israel, and with the house of Judah: . . .

But this shall be the covenant that I will make with the house of Israel; After those days, saith the Lord,

I will put my law in their inward parts, and write it in their hearts; and will be their God, and they shall be my people. [Jeremiah 31:1, 31, 33]

[Lord God/Ezekiel] Thus shall they know that I the Lord their God am with them, and that they, even the house of Israel, are my people, saith the Lord God. [Ezekiel 34:30]

[Joseph Smith] Trusting in that God who has said that these things are hid from the wise and prudent, and revealed unto babes, I step forth into the field to tell you what the Lord is doing, and what you must do. . . .

The time has at last arrived when the God of Abraham, of Isaac, and of Jacob, has set His hand again the second time to recover the remnants of his people, . . . and establish that covenant with them, which was promised when their sins should be taken away. See Isaiah 11, Romans 11:25, 26 and 27, and also Jeremiah 31:31, 32 and 33. This covenant has never been established with the house of Israel, nor with the house of Judah, for it requires two parties to make a covenant, and those two parties must be agreed, or no covenant can be made.

Christ, in the days of His flesh, proposed to make a covenant with them, but they rejected Him and His proposals, and in consequence thereof, they were broken off, and no covenant was made with them at that time. But their unbelief has not rendered the promise of God of none effect: no, for there was another day . . . [when] His people, Israel, should be a willing people;—and He would write His law in their hearts, and print it in their thoughts; their sins and their iniquities He would remember no more.

Thus after this chosen family had rejected Christ and His proposals, the heralds of salvation said to them, "Lo, we turn unto the Gentiles;" and the Gentiles received the covenant, and were grafted in from whence the chosen family were broken off: but

> the Gentiles have not continued in the goodness of God, but have departed from the faith that was once delivered to the Saints, and have broken the covenant in which their fathers were established (see Isaiah 24:5); and have become high-minded, and have not feared; therefore, but few of them will be gathered with the chosen family. . . .
>
> And now what remains to be done, under circumstances like these? I will proceed to tell you what the Lord requires of all people, high and low, rich and poor, male and female, ministers and people, professors of religion and non-professors, in order that they may enjoy the Holy Spirit of God to a fulness and escape the judgments of God, which are almost ready to burst upon the nations of the earth. Repent of all your sins, and be baptized in water for the remission of them, in the name of the Father, and of the Son, and of the Holy Ghost, and receive the ordinance of the laying on of the hands of him who is ordained and sealed unto this power, that ye may receive the Holy Spirit of God; and this is according to the Holy Scriptures.[3]

Joseph Smith knew that he would be an instrument in the hands of the Lord in helping to restore ancient and yet new and everlasting covenants, including the ordinances of baptism by immersion for the remission of sins and of the reception of the sanctifying powers of the gift of the Holy Ghost.

> [Lord through Paul] Behold, the days come, saith the Lord, when I will make a new covenant with the house of Israel and with the house of Judah:
>
> Not according to the covenant that I made with their fathers in the day when I took them by the hand to lead them out of the land of Egypt; because they continued not in my covenant, and I regarded them not, saith the Lord.
>
> For this is the covenant that I will make with the

house of Israel after those days, saith the Lord; I will put my laws into their mind, and write them in their hearts: and I will be to them a God, and they shall be to me a people. [Hebrews 8:8–10]

[Lord God concerning Joseph Smith] For thus saith the Lord God: Him have I inspired to move the cause of Zion in mighty power for good, and his diligence I know, and his prayers I have heard.

Yea, his weeping for Zion I have seen, and I will cause that he shall mourn for her no longer; for his days of rejoicing are come unto the remission of his sins, and the manifestations of my blessings upon his works. [D&C 21:7–8)]

[Joseph Smith] On the evening of the 21st of September, A.D. 1823, while I was praying unto God, and endeavoring to exercise faith in the precious promises of Scripture, on a sudden a light like that of day, only of a far purer and more glorious appearance and brightness, burst into the room, indeed the first sight was as though the house was filled with consuming fire; the appearance produced a shock that affected the whole body; in a moment a personage stood before me surrounded with a glory yet greater than that with which I was already surrounded. This messenger proclaimed himself to be an angel of God, sent to bring the joyful tidings that the covenant which God made with ancient Israel was at hand to be fulfilled, that the preparatory work for the second coming of the Messiah was speedily to commence; that the time was at hand for the Gospel in all its fulness to be preached in power, unto all nations that a people might be prepared for the Millennial reign. I was informed that I was chosen to be an instrument in the hands of God to bring about some of His purposes in this glorious dispensation.

I was also informed concerning the aboriginal inhabitants of this country and shown who they were, and from whence they came.[4]

> [Lehi] And there shall rise up one mighty among them, who shall do much good, both in word and in deed, being an instrument in the hands of God, with exceeding faith, to work mighty wonders, and do that thing which is great in the sight of God, unto the bringing to pass much restoration unto the house of Israel, and unto the seed of thy brethren. [2 Nephi 3:24]

> [Brigham Young] It was decreed in the councils of eternity, long before the foundations of the earth were laid, that he [Joseph Smith] should be the man in the last dispensation of this world, to bring forth the word of God to this people, and receive the fulness of the keys and power of the Priesthood of the Son of God. The Lord had his eye upon him, and upon his father, and upon his father's father, and upon their progenitors clear back to Abraham, and from Abraham to the flood, from the flood to Enoch, and from Enoch to Adam. He has watched that family and that blood as it has circulated from its fountain to the birth of that man. He [Joseph Smith] was foreordained in eternity to preside over this last dispensation.[5]

Joseph Smith and his associate Oliver Cowdery received from John the Baptist and later from Peter, James, and John the keys of the priesthood necessary to establish the kingdom of God upon the earth and to administer the earlier covenants and ordinances of the gospel.

> [John the Baptist] Upon you my fellow servants, in the name of Messiah I confer the Priesthood of Aaron, which holds the keys of the ministering of angels, and of the gospel of repentance, and of baptism by immersion for the remission of sins; and this shall never be taken again from the earth, until the sons of Levi do offer again an offering unto the Lord in righteousness. [D&C 13:1]

Joseph Smith and his associate Oliver Cowdery received from Moses, from Elias, and from Elijah those keys of the priesthood necessary to fulfill the promises of the Lord to the descendants of his ancient covenant people. These appearances were in fulfillment of prophecies in Malachi 4:4–6, 3 Nephi 24 and 25, Doctrine and Covenants 133:64, and Joseph Smith–History 1:36–39.

> [Lord of Hosts/Malachi] Behold, I will send you Elijah the prophet before the coming of the great and dreadful day of the Lord:
>
> And he shall turn the heart of the fathers to the children, and the heart of the children to their fathers, lest I come and smite the earth with a curse. [Malachi 4:5–6]

> [Lord through angel Moroni to Joseph Smith] Behold, I will reveal unto you the Priesthood, by the hand of Elijah the prophet, before the coming of the great and dreadful day of the Lord.
>
> And he shall plant in the hearts of the children the promises made to the fathers, and the hearts of the children shall turn to their fathers.
>
> If it were not so, the whole earth would be utterly wasted at his coming. [D&C 2:1–3]

> [Joseph Smith and Oliver Cowdery] After this vision closed, the heavens were again opened unto us; and Moses appeared before us, and committed unto us the keys of the gathering of Israel from the four parts of the earth, and the leading of the ten tribes from the land of the north.
>
> After this, Elias appeared, and committed the dispensation of the gospel of Abraham, saying that in us and our seed all generations after us should be blessed.
>
> After this vision had closed, another great and glorious vision burst upon us; for Elijah the prophet, who was taken to heaven without tasting death, stood before us, and said:
>
> Behold, the time has fully come, which was spoken

> of by the mouth of Malachi—testifying that he [Elijah] should be sent, before the great and dreadful day of the Lord come—
>
> To turn the hearts of the fathers to the children, and the children to the fathers, lest the whole earth be smitten with a curse—
>
> Therefore, the keys of this dispensation are committed into your hands; and by this ye may know that the great and dreadful day of the Lord is near, even at the doors. [D&C 110:11–16]

Joseph Smith, under the inspiration of the Lord, continued to exercise these keys in behalf of the kingdom of God upon the earth.

> [Daniel] Daniel answered in the presence of the king, . . .
>
> But there is a God in heaven that revealeth secrets, and maketh known to the king Nebuchadnezzar what shall be in the latter days. Thy dream, and the visions of thy head upon thy bed, are these;
>
> As for thee, O king, thy thoughts came into thy mind upon thy bed, what should come to pass hereafter: and he that revealeth secrets maketh known to thee what shall come to pass. . . .
>
> Thou sawest till that a stone was cut out without hands, which smote the image upon his feet that were of iron and clay, and brake them to pieces.
>
> Then was the iron, the clay, the brass, the silver, and the gold, broken to pieces together, and became like the chaff of the summer threshingfloors; and the wind carried them away, that no place was found for them: and the stone that smote the image became a great mountain, and filled the whole earth. [Daniel 2:27–29, 34–35]

> [Daniel] And in the days of these kings shall the God of heaven set up a kingdom, which shall never be destroyed: and the kingdom shall not be left to other people, but it shall break in pieces and consume all

> these kingdoms, and it shall stand for ever. [Daniel 2:44]

Joseph Smith established the first formally organized mission of the Church in 1837 in the British Isles, the exact region into which many of the blood of Israel had been scattered by the Romans. The hearts of the prophets of the dispensation of the fulness of times started to be turned toward the Jews and toward all the descendants of the house of Israel.

> [Lord to Church] Therefore, . . . seek diligently to turn the hearts of the children to their fathers, and the hearts of the fathers to the children;
>
> And again, the hearts of the Jews unto the prophets, and the prophets unto the Jews; lest I come and smite the whole earth with a curse, and all flesh be consumed before me. [D&C 98:16–17]

Joseph Smith in 1841 set apart two of the apostles of The Church of Jesus Christ of Latter-day Saints, Orson Hyde and John E. Page, to go to the ancient covenant land of Israel and to dedicate that land for the return of the Jews.

> [Joseph Smith] I am happy in being informed by your letter that your mission swells "larger and larger." It is a great and important mission, and one that is worthy [of] those intelligences who surround the throne of Jehovah to be engaged in. Although it appears great at present, yet you have but just begun to realize the greatness, the extent and glory of the same. If there is anything calculated to interest the mind of the Saints, to awaken in them the finest sensibilities, and arouse them to enterprise and exertion, surely it is the great and precious promises made by our heavenly Father to the children of Abraham; and those engaged in seeking the outcasts of Israel, and the dispersed of Judah, cannot fail to enjoy the Spirit of

> the Lord and have the choicest blessings of heaven rest upon them in copious effusions.
>
> Brethren, you are in the pathway to eternal fame, and immortal glory; and inasmuch as you feel interested for the covenant people of the Lord, the God of their fathers shall bless you. Do not be discouraged on account of the greatness of the work; only be humble and faithful, . . . He who scattered Israel has promised to gather them; therefore inasmuch as you are to be instrumental in this great work, He will endow you with power, wisdom, might and intelligence, and every qualification necessary; while your minds will expand wider and wider, until you can circumscribe the earth and the heavens, reach forth into eternity, and contemplate the mighty acts of Jehovah in all their variety and glory.[6]

> [Orson Hyde] [I] dedicate and consecrate this land unto Thee, for the gathering together of Judah's scattered remnants, according to the predictions of the holy Prophets. . . .
>
> . . . Incline them to gather in upon this land according to Thy word. Let them come like clouds and like doves to their windows. Let the large ships of the nations bring them from the distant isles; and let kings become their nursing fathers, and queens with motherly fondness wipe the tear of sorrow from their eyes.[7]

Joseph Smith began building a temple in Nauvoo, Illinois, and by 1846, within eighteen months after his martyrdom, it was complete enough that sections could be dedicated so that sacred covenants could once again be administered. Truly, the blood of Israel started to be gathered again into covenant Israel. The hearts of the fathers turned toward their children, and the hearts of the children to their fathers.

> [Joseph Smith] The Bible says, "I will send you Elijah the Prophet before the coming of the great and

> dreadful day of the Lord; and he shall turn the hearts of the fathers to the children, and the hearts of the children to the fathers, lest I come and smite the earth with a curse" [Malachi 4:5–6].
>
> Now, the word *turn* here should be translated *bind,* or seal. But what is the object of this important mission? or how is it to be fulfilled? The keys are to be delivered, the spirit of Elijah is to come, the Gospel to be established, the Saints of God gathered, Zion built up, and the Saints to come up as saviors on Mount Zion.[8]

By 1948 an independent nation called Israel had been established on the earth, and the blood of a special section of the house of Israel returned with fervor to the lands of ancient covenant Israel.

> [Lord God of Hosts/Nephi, son of Lehi] And it shall come to pass that my people, which are of the house of Israel, shall be gathered home unto the lands of their possessions; and my word also shall be gathered in one. And I will show unto them that fight against my word and against my people, who are of the house of Israel, that I am God, and that I covenanted with Abraham that I would remember his seed forever. [2 Nephi 29:14]

> [Nephi, son of Lehi] And it shall come to pass that the Jews which are scattered also shall begin to believe in Christ; and they shall begin to gather in upon the face of the land; and as many as shall believe in Christ shall also become a delightsome people.
>
> And it shall come to pass that the Lord God shall commence his work among all nations, kindreds, tongues, and people, to bring about the restoration of his people upon the earth. [2 Nephi 30:7–8]

> [Lord God/Ezekiel] And I will make them one nation in the land upon the mountains of Israel; and one king shall be king to them all: and they shall be

> no more two nations, neither shall they be divided into two kingdoms any more at all. [Ezekiel 37:22]

Most of the preceding points have been concerned with the origin and history of the house of Israel, but what of the prophesied destiny of the house of Israel? The points that follow will be just as certain and as definite as those that are part of the historical past and of the present. Remember the elements included in the definition of *destiny* cited above: "condition foreordained by divine will" and "the predetermined course of events . . . ; the foreordained future."

The Lord revealed through Isaiah:

> [God/Isaiah] Remember the former things of old: for I am God, and there is none else; I am God, and there is none like me,
>
> Declaring the end from the beginning, and from ancient times the things that are not yet done, saying, My counsel shall stand, and I will do all my pleasure. [Isaiah 46:9–10]

THE TRUTHS OF THE HOUSE OF ISRAEL "AS THEY WILL BE"

What of the future?

The descendants of Judah of the house of Israel will continue to return to their lands of inheritance. This endeavor will continue to so excite and concern other nations on the earth that they will fight against Judah.

> [Lord/Zechariah] Behold, the day of the Lord cometh, and thy spoil shall be divided in the midst of thee.
>
> For I will gather all nations against Jerusalem to battle; and the city shall be taken, and the houses rifled, and the women ravished; and half of the city

> shall go forth into captivity, and the residue of the people shall not be cut off from the city. [Zechariah 14:1–2]
>
> [Jesus Christ] And in that day shall be heard of wars and rumors of wars, and the whole earth shall be in commotion, and men's hearts shall fail them, and they shall say that Christ delayeth his coming until the end of the earth.
>
> And the love of men shall wax cold, and iniquity shall abound. [D&C 45:26–27]
>
> [Wilford Woodruff, 22 February 1879] O house of Judah. . . . It is true that after you return and gather your nation home, and rebuild your City and Temple, that the Gentiles may gather together their armies to go against you to battle, to take you a prey and to take you as a spoil, which they will do, for the words of your prophets must be fulfilled.[9]

The descendants of Ephraim, and thus of Joseph, will continue to carry the "good news" of the gospel throughout the earth and will build holy houses to the Lord where conditions and need merit.

> [Lord] Send forth the elders of my church unto the nations which are afar off; unto the islands of the sea; send forth unto foreign lands; call upon all nations, first upon the Gentiles, and then upon the Jews. [D&C 133:8]
>
> [Lord to James Covill, a former Baptist minister] And if thou do this, I have prepared thee for a greater work. Thou shalt preach the fulness of my gospel, which I have sent forth in these last days, the covenant which I have sent forth to recover my people, which are of the house of Israel. [D&C 39:11]
>
> [Jesus] And this gospel of the kingdom shall be preached in all the world for a witness unto all nations; and then shall the end come. [Matthew 24:14]

> [Jesus Christ] Wherefore, I must bring forth the fulness of my gospel from the Gentiles unto the house of Israel. [D&C 14:10]
>
> [Lord] And they shall be filled with songs of everlasting joy.
>
> Behold, this is the blessing of the everlasting God upon the tribes of Israel, and the richer blessing upon the head of Ephraim and his fellows.
>
> And they also of the tribe of Judah, after their pain, shall be sanctified in holiness before the Lord, to dwell in his presence day and night, forever and ever. [D&C 133:33–35]
>
> [Joseph Smith] In speaking of the gathering, we mean to be understood as speaking of it according to scripture, the gathering of the elect of the Lord out of every nation on earth, and bringing them to the place of the Lord of Hosts, when the city of righteousness shall be built, and where the people shall be of one heart and one mind . . . where even upon the bells of the horses shall be written *"Holiness to the Lord."*
>
> The Book of Mormon has made known who Israel is, upon this continent.[10]

Eventually—and this is clearly in the future—the message of the fulness of the gospel of Jesus Christ will be taken to the blood of the house of Israel living in the land of Israel. Thus we read these prophetic words of the resurrected Jesus Christ himself:

> [Jesus Christ] And I will remember the covenant which I have made with my people; and I have covenanted with them that I would gather them together in mine own due time, that I would give unto them again the land of their fathers for their inheritance, which is the land of Jerusalem, which is the promised land unto them forever, saith the Father.
>
> And it shall come to pass that the time cometh,

when the fulness of my gospel shall be preached unto them;

And they shall believe in me, that I am Jesus Christ, the Son of God, and shall pray unto the Father in my name.

Then shall their watchmen lift up their voice, and with the voice together shall they sing; for they shall see eye to eye.

Then will the Father gather them together again, and give unto them Jerusalem for the land of their inheritance.

Then shall they break forth into joy—Sing together, ye waste places of Jerusalem; for the Father hath comforted his people, he hath redeemed Jerusalem.

The Father hath made bare his holy arm in the eyes of all the nations; and all the ends of the earth shall see the salvation of the Father; and the Father and I are one. [3 Nephi 20:29–35]

[Mormon] Now these things are written unto the remnant of the house of Jacob; and they are written after this manner, because it is known of God that wickedness will not bring them forth unto them; and they are to be hid up unto the Lord that they may come forth in his own due time.

And this is the commandment which I have received; and behold, they shall come forth according to the commandment of the Lord, when he shall see fit, in his wisdom.

And behold, they [the writings in the Book of Mormon] shall go unto the unbelieving of the Jews; and for this intent shall they go—that they may be persuaded that Jesus is the Christ, the Son of the living God; that the Father may bring about, through his most Beloved, his great and eternal purpose, in restoring the Jews, or all the house of Israel, to the land of their inheritance, which the Lord their God hath given them, unto the fulfilling of his covenant. [Mormon 5:12–14]

> [Jesus Christ/Moroni] Come unto me, O ye house of Israel, and it shall be made manifest unto you how great things the Father hath laid up for you, from the foundation of the world; and it hath not come unto you, because of unbelief.
>
> Behold, when ye shall rend that veil of unbelief which doth cause you to remain in your awful state of wickedness, and hardness of heart, and blindness of mind, then shall the great and marvelous things which have been hid up from the foundation of the world from you—yea, when ye shall call upon the Father in my name, with a broken heart and a contrite spirit, then shall ye know that the Father hath remembered the covenant which he made unto your fathers, O house of Israel. [Ether 4:14–15]

> [Wilford Woodruff, 25 February 1855] When the Gentiles reject the gospel it will be taken from them, and go to the house of Israel, to that long suffering people that are now scattered abroad through all the nations upon the earth, . . . and they will rebuild Jerusalem their ancient city, and make it more glorious than at the beginning, and they will have a leader in Israel with them, a man that is full of the power of God and the gift of the Holy Ghost; but they are held now from this work, only because the fulness of the Gentiles has not yet come in.[11]

As part of this preaching of the gospel of Jesus Christ to the blood of Israel in Judah, two prophets will be sent to Jerusalem. After three and a half years these prophets will be killed.

> [John the Revelator] For it [the court which is without the temple] is given unto the Gentiles: and the holy city shall they tread under foot forty and two months.
>
> And I will give power unto my two witnesses, and they shall prophesy a thousand two hundred and threescore days, clothed in sackcloth. . . .

These have power to shut heaven, that it rain not in the days of their prophecy: and have power over waters to turn them to blood, and to smite the earth with all plagues, as often as they will.

And when they shall have finished their testimony, the beast that ascendeth out of the bottomless pit shall make war against them, and shall overcome them, and kill them.

And their dead bodies shall lie in the street of the great city, which spiritually is called Sodom and Egypt, where also our Lord was crucified.

And they of the people and kindreds and tongues and nations shall see their dead bodies three days and an half, and shall not suffer their dead bodies to be put in graves.

And they that dwell upon the earth shall rejoice over them, and make merry, and shall send gifts one to another; because these two prophets tormented them that dwelt on the earth.

And after three days and an half the Spirit of life from God entered into them, and they stood upon their feet; and great fear fell upon them which saw them.

And they heard a great voice from heaven saying unto them, Come up hither. And they ascended up to heaven in a cloud; and their enemies beheld them. [Revelation 11:2–3, 6–12]

[Inspiration of Joseph Smith] Q. What is to be understood by the two witnesses, in the eleventh chapter of Revelation?

A. They are two prophets that are to be raised up to the Jewish nation in the last days, at the time of the restoration, and to prophesy to the Jews after they are gathered and have built the city of Jerusalem in the land of their fathers. [D&C 77:15]

[Testimony of Elder LeGrand Richards concerning these prophets] No doubt these prophets will be called and ordained and sent by the First Presidency of The

Church of Jesus Christ of Latter-day Saints, for the Lord's house is a house of order, and true prophets are never self sent—they must be called and sent of God.[12]

As part of the preparation and sanctifying of the land, a temple will be built in Jerusalem.

[Lord of Hosts/Zechariah] Thus saith the Lord of hosts; Behold, I will save my people from the east country, and from the west country;

And I will bring them, and they shall dwell in the midst of Jerusalem: and they shall be my people, and I will be their God, in truth and in righteousness.

Thus saith the Lord of hosts; Let your hands be strong, ye that hear in these days these words by the mouth of the prophets, which were in the day that the foundation of the house of the Lord of hosts was laid, that the temple might be built. [Zechariah 8:7–9]

[Lord] For it is ordained that in Zion, and in her stakes, and in Jerusalem, those places which I have appointed for refuge, shall be the places for your baptisms for your dead.

And again, verily I say unto you, how shall your washings be acceptable unto me, except ye perform them in a house which you have built to my name? [D&C 124:36–37]

[Joseph Smith, 11 June 1843] What was the object of gathering the Jews, or the people of God in any age of the world? . . . The main object was to build unto the Lord a house whereby He could reveal unto His people the ordinances of His house and the glories of His kingdom, and teach the people the way of salvation; for there are certain ordinances and principles that, when they are taught and practiced, must be done in a place or house built for that purpose.[13]

[Joseph Smith] It was the design of the councils of heaven before the world was, that the principles and laws of the priesthood should be predicated upon the gathering of the people in every age of the world. Jesus did everything to gather the people, and they would not be gathered, and He therefore poured out curses upon them. Ordinances instituted in the heavens before the foundation of the world, in the priesthood, for the salvation of men, are not to be altered or changed. All must be saved on the same principles.

It is for the same purpose that God gathers together his people in the last days, to build unto the Lord a house to prepare them for the ordinances and endowments, washings and anointings, etc. One of the ordinances of the house of the Lord is baptism for the dead. God decreed before the foundation of the world that that ordinance should be administered in a font prepared for that purpose in the house of the Lord.[14]

Water will issue forth from under the temple (the house of the Lord) and flow into the Dead Sea, whose waters will be healed and will contain "the fish of the great sea."

[Ezekiel/Lord God] Afterward he [the Lord] brought me again unto the door of the house; and, behold, waters issued out from under the threshold of the house eastward: for the forefront of the house stood toward the east, and the waters came down from under from the right side of the house, at the south side of the altar.

Then brought he me out of the way of the gate northward, and led me about the way without unto the utter gate by the way that looketh eastward; and, behold, there ran out waters on the right side.

And when the man that had the line in his hand went forth eastward, he measured a thousand cubits, and he brought me through the waters; the waters were to the ankles.

Again he measured a thousand, and brought me through the waters; the waters were to the knees.

> Again he measured a thousand, and brought me through; the waters were to the loins.
>
> Afterward he measured a thousand; and it was a river that I could not pass over: for the waters were risen, waters to swim in, a river that could not be passed over.
>
> And he said unto me, Son of man, hast thou seen this? Then he brought me, and caused me to return to the brink of the river.
>
> Now when I had returned, behold, at the bank of the river were very many trees on the one side and on the other.
>
> Then said he unto me, These waters issue out toward the east country, and go down into the desert, and go into the sea: which being brought forth into the sea, the waters shall be healed.
>
> And it shall come to pass, that every thing that liveth, which moveth, whithersoever the rivers shall come, shall live: and there shall be a very great multitude of fish, because these waters shall come thither: for they shall be healed; and every thing shall live whither the river cometh.
>
> And it shall come to pass, that the fishers shall stand upon it from En-gedi even unto En-eglaim; they shall be a place to spread forth nets; their fish shall be according to their kinds, as the fish of the great sea, exceeding many.
>
> But the miry places thereof and the marshes thereof shall not be healed; they shall be given to salt.
>
> And by the river upon the bank thereof, on this side and on that side, shall grow all trees for meat, whose leaf shall not fade, neither shall the fruit thereof be consumed: it shall bring forth new fruit according to his months, because their waters they issued out of the sanctuary: and the fruit thereof shall be for meat, and the leaf thereof for medicine. [Ezekiel 47:1–12]
>
> [Joseph Smith, 6 April 1843] Judah must return, Jerusalem must be rebuilt, and the temple, and water

come out from under the temple, and the waters of the Dead Sea be healed. It will take some time to rebuild the walls of the city and the temple, etc.; and all this must be done before the Son of Man will make His appearance.[15]

A leader named David, a descendant of the loins of ancient David, will become a king, a shepherd, and a prince in Israel. This leader is mentioned in Jeremiah 23:38; 30:3–9; Ezekiel 34:23–24, 28; 37:24–25; Isaiah 55:3–4; Hosea 3:4–5; Zechariah 3:8–9; 6:11–13.

[Lord God/Ezekiel] Thus saith the Lord God; Behold, I will take the children of Israel from among the heathen, whither they be gone, and will gather them on every side, and bring them into their own land:

And I will make them one nation in the land upon the mountains of Israel; and one king shall be king to them all: and they shall be no more two nations, neither shall they be divided into two kingdoms any more at all:

Neither shall they defile themselves any more with their idols, nor with their detestable things, nor with any of their transgressions: but I will save them out of all their dwellingplaces, wherein they have sinned, and will cleanse them: so shall they be my people, and I will be their God.

And David my servant shall be king over them; and they all shall have one shepherd: they shall also walk in my judgments, and observe my statutes, and do them.

And they shall dwell in the land that I have given unto Jacob my servant, wherein your fathers have dwelt; and they shall dwell therein, even they, and their children, and their children's children for ever: and my servant David shall be their prince for ever. [Ezekiel 37:21–25]

[Joseph Smith] The throne and kingdom of David

> is to be taken from him and given to another by the name of David in the last days, raised up out of his lineage.[16]

> [Orson Hyde] Let them know that it is Thy good pleasure to restore the kingdom unto Israel—raise up Jerusalem as its capital, and constitute her people a distinct nation and government, with David Thy servant, even a descendant from the loins of ancient David to be their king.[17]

Then, as a confirming sign to the blood of Israel living in the land of Israel, their Messiah will appear to them, declaring that he is indeed the Messiah, even Jesus Christ, the Son of God. A "nation," the descendants of the house of Israel then living in Israel, will "be born at once," that is, converted to the Lord and to his gospel.

> [Lord/Isaiah] Who hath heard such a thing? who hath seen such things? Shall the earth be made to bring forth in one day? or shall a nation be born at once? for as soon as Zion travailed, she brought forth her children. [Isaiah 66:8]

> [Lord of Hosts/Zechariah] And I will pour upon the house of David, and upon the inhabitants of Jerusalem, the spirit of grace and of supplications: and they shall look upon me whom they have pierced, and they shall mourn for him, as one mourneth for his only son, and shall be in bitterness for him, as one that is in bitterness for his firstborn. [Zechariah 12:10]

> [Lord of Hosts/Zechariah] And one shall say unto him, What are these wounds in thine hands? Then he shall answer, Those with which I was wounded in the house of my friends. [Zechariah 13:6]

> [Jesus Christ] And then shall the Jews look upon me and say: What are these wounds in thine hands and in thy feet?
>
> Then shall they know that I am the Lord; for I will say unto them: These wounds are the wounds with

> which I was wounded in the house of my friends. I am he who was lifted up. I am Jesus that was crucified. I am the Son of God.
>
> And then shall they weep because of their iniquities; then shall they lament because they persecuted their king. [D&C 45:51–53]

Jesus Christ will then lead the armies of Israel to victory over the combined armies of the nations of the earth.

> [Zechariah] Then shall the Lord go forth, and fight against those nations, as when he fought in the day of battle. . . .
>
> And the Lord shall be king over all the earth: in that day shall there be one Lord and his name one. [Zechariah 14:3, 9]

> [Wilford Woodruff, January 1873] The Jews have got to gather to their own land in unbelief . . . and when they have done this and rebuilt their city, the Gentiles, in fulfillment of the words of Ezekiel, Jeremiah and other prophets, will go up against Jerusalem to battle and to take a spoil and a prey; and then when they have taken one-half of Jerusalem captive and distressed the Jews for the last time on the earth, their Great Deliverer, Shiloh, will come.[18]

Then comes the completion of the destiny of the house of Israel, leading up to the great millennial reign of Jesus Christ upon the earth as King of kings and Lord of lords. In preparation for this great day, two world capitals must be prepared as prophesied—one in "Zion" and one in Jerusalem.

> [Isaiah] And it shall come to pass in the last days, that the mountain of the Lord's house shall be established in the top of the mountains, and shall be exalted above the hills; and all nations shall flow unto it.
>
> And many people shall go and say, Come ye, and let us go up to the mountain of the Lord, to the house

of the God of Jacob; and he will teach us of his ways, and we will walk in his paths: for out of Zion shall go forth the law, and the word of the Lord from Jerusalem. [Isaiah 2:2–3]

[Lord] Wherefore, prepare ye for the coming of the Bridegroom; go ye, go ye out to meet him.

For behold, he shall stand upon the mount of Olivet, and upon the mighty ocean, even the great deep, and upon the islands of the sea, and upon the land of Zion.

And he shall utter his voice out of Zion, and he shall speak from Jerusalem, and his voice shall be heard among all people. [D&C 133:19–21]

[Jesus Christ] And they shall assist my people, the remnant of Jacob, and also as many of the house of Israel as shall come, that they may build a city, which shall be called the New Jerusalem. [3 Nephi 21:23]

[Ether/Moroni] And he spake also concerning the house of Israel, and the Jerusalem from whence Lehi should come—after it should be destroyed it should be built up again, a holy city unto the Lord; wherefore, it could not be a new Jerusalem for it had been in a time of old; but it should be built up again, and become a holy city of the Lord; and it should be built unto the house of Israel. [Ether 13:5]

[Ether/Moroni] And then cometh the New Jerusalem; and blessed are they who dwell therein, for it is they whose garments are white through the blood of the Lamb; and they are they who are numbered among the remnant of the seed of Joseph, who were of the house of Israel. [Ether 13:10]

[Joseph Smith] The Book of Mormon is a record of the forefathers of our western tribes of Indians; . . . [who] are descendants from that Joseph who was sold into Egypt, . . . the land of America is a promised land unto them, and unto it all the tribes of Israel will come, with as many of the Gentiles as shall comply with the requisitions of the new covenant. . . . The city of Zion spoken of by David, in the one hundred and second Psalm, will be built upon the land of America. . . . But Judah shall obtain deliverance at Jerusalem. . . . These are testimonies that the Good Shepherd will put forth His own sheep, and lead them out from all nations where they have been scattered in a cloudy and dark day, to Zion, and to Jerusalem.[19]

[Joseph Smith] I received, by a heavenly vision, a commandment in June following, to take my journey to the western boundaries of the State of Missouri, and there designate the very spot which was to be the central place for the commencement of the gathering together of those who embrace the fullness of the everlasting Gospel. Accordingly I undertook the journey, with certain ones of my brethren, and after a long and tedious journey, suffering many privations and hardships, arrived in Jackson County, Missouri, and after viewing the country, seeking diligently at the hand of God, He manifested Himself unto us, . . . and designed to commence the work of the gathering, and the upbuilding of an "holy city," which should be called Zion—. . .

Now we learn from the Book of Mormon the very identical continent and spot of land upon which the New Jerusalem is to stand, and it must be caught up according to the vision of John upon the isle of Patmos.

Now many will feel disposed to say, that this New Jerusalem spoken of, is the Jerusalem that was built by the Jews on the eastern continent. But you will see, from Revelations 21:2, there was a New Jerusalem coming down from God out of heaven, adorned as a bride for her husband; that after this, the Revelator was caught away in the Spirit, to a great and high mountain, and saw the great and holy city descending out of heaven from God. Now there are two cities spoken of here. . . there is a New Jerusalem to be

> established on this continent, and also Jerusalem shall be rebuilt on the eastern continent.[20]
>
> [Joseph Fielding Smith] Jerusalem of old, after the Jews have been cleansed and sanctified from all their sins, shall become a holy city where the Lord shall dwell and from whence he shall send forth his word unto all people. Likewise, on this continent, the city of Zion, New Jerusalem—shall be built, and from it the law of God shall also go forth. [See D&C 45:66–67; 84:2.] There will be no conflict, for each city shall be headquarters for the Redeemer of the world, and from each he shall send forth his proclamations as occasion may require. Jerusalem shall be the gathering place of Judah and his fellows of the house of Israel, and Zion shall be the gathering place of Ephraim and his fellows, upon whose heads shall be conferred "the richer blessings" [see D&C 133:34].[21]

Eventually the resurrected Messiah, Jesus Christ, and his apostles will judge "the whole house of Israel."

> [Jesus Christ] For behold, I shall speak unto the Jews and they shall write it; and I shall also speak unto the Nephites and they shall write it; and I shall also speak unto the other tribes of the house of Israel, which I have led away, and they shall write it; and I shall also speak unto all nations of the earth and they shall write it. [D&C 29:12]
>
> [Daniel] I saw in the night visions, and, behold, one like the Son of man came with the clouds of heaven, and came to the Ancient of days, and they brought him near before him.
>
> And there was given him dominion, and glory, and a kingdom, that all people, nations, and languages, should serve him: his dominion is an everlasting dominion, which shall not pass away, and his kingdom that which shall not be destroyed. [Daniel 7:13–14]

SUMMARY

The prophet Wilford Woodruff reflected upon these teachings:

> The Lord has decreed that the Jews should be gathered from all the Gentile nations where they have been driven, into their own land, in fulfillment of the words of Moses their law-giver. And this is the will of your great Eloheim, O house of Judah, and whenever you shall be called upon to perform this work, the God of Israel will help you. You have a great future and destiny before you and you cannot avoid fulfilling it; you are the royal chosen seed, and the God of your father's house has kept you distinct as a nation. . . . You may not wait until you believe on Jesus of Nazareth, but when you meet with Shiloh your king, you will know him; your destiny is marked out, you cannot avoid it. . . . It is true that after you return and gather your nation home, and rebuild your City and Temple, that the Gentiles may gather together their armies to go against you to battle, to take you a prey and to take you as a spoil, which they will do, for the words of your prophets must be fulfilled; but when this affliction comes, the living God, that led Moses through the wilderness, will deliver you, and your Shiloh will come and stand in your midst and will fight your battles; and you will know him, and the afflictions of the Jews will be at an end, while the destruction of the Gentiles will be so great that it will take the whole house of Israel who are gathered about Jerusalem, seven months to bury the dead of their enemies, and the weapons of war will last them seven years for fuel, so that they need not go to any forest for wood. These are tremendous sayings—who can bear them? Nevertheless they are true, and will be fulfilled, according to the sayings of Ezekiel, Zechariah, and other prophets. Though the heavens and the earth pass away, not one jot or tittle will fall unfulfilled. [22 Feb. 1879][22]

And feeling the spirit of this great work of the last days, the Prophet Joseph Smith exclaimed:

> The building up of Zion is a cause that has interested the people of God in every age; it is a theme upon which prophets, priests and kings have dwelt with peculiar delight; they have looked forward with joyful anticipation to the day in which we live; and fired with heavenly and joyful anticipations they have sung and written and prophesied of this our day; but they died without the sight; we are the favored people that God has made choice of to bring about the Latter-day glory; it is left for us to see, participate in and help to roll forward the Latter-day glory, "the dispensation of the fulness of times, when God will gather together all things that are in heaven, and all things that are upon the earth," "even in one," when the Saints of God will be gathered in one from every nation, and kindred, and people, and tongue, when the Jews will be gathered together into one, the wicked will also be gathered together to be destroyed, as spoken of by the prophets; the Spirit of God will also dwell with His people, and be withdrawn from the rest of the nations, and all things whether in heaven or on earth will be in one, even in Christ. The heavenly Priesthood will unite with the earthly, to bring about those great purposes; and whilst we are thus united in one common cause, to roll forth the kingdom of God, the heavenly Priesthood are not idle spectators, the Spirit of God will be showered down from above, and it will dwell in our midst. The blessings of the Most High will rest upon our tabernacles, and our name will be handed down to future ages; our children will rise up and call us blessed; and generations yet unborn will dwell with peculiar delight upon the scenes that we have passed through, the privations that we have endured; the untiring zeal that we have manifested; the all but insurmountable difficulties that we have overcome in

> laying the foundation of a work that brought about the glory and blessing which they will realize; a work that God and angels have contemplated with delight for generations past; that fired the souls of the ancient patriarchs and prophets; a work that is destined to bring about the destruction of the powers of darkness, the renovation of the earth, the glory of God, and the salvation of the human family. [2 May 1842][23]
>
> [Joseph Smith] Brethren, shall we not go on in so great a cause? Go forward and not backward. Courage, brethren; and on, on to the victory. [D&C 128:22]

I pray that we may do our small part in the cause of teaching and advancing this great work.

NOTES

1. James Strong, *The Exhaustive Concordance of the Bible* (Nashville, Tenn.: Abingdon Press, 1894).

2. R. Gary Shapiro, comp., *An Exhaustive Concordance of the Book of Mormon, Doctrine and Covenants, and Pearl of Great Price* (Salt Lake City: Hawkes Publishing, 1977), [iv].

3. Joseph Smith, *History of The Church of Jesus Christ of Latter-day Saints,* 7 vols., 2d. ed. rev., ed. B. H. Roberts (Salt Lake City: The Church of Jesus Christ of Latter-day Saints, 1932–51), 1:313–14.

4. Smith, *History of the Church,* 4:536–37.

5. In *Journal of Discourses,* 26 vols. (London: Latter-day Saints' Book Depot, 1854–86), 7:289–90.

6. Joseph Smith, *Teachings of the Prophet Joseph Smith,* sel. Joseph Fielding Smith (Salt Lake City: Deseret Book, 1978), 163.

7. In N. B. Lundwall, comp., *Temples of the Most High,* 5th ed. (Salt Lake City: N. B. Lundwall, 1945), 219–20.

8. Smith, *History of the Church,* 6:183–84.

9. Matthew Cowley, *Wilford Woodruff* (Salt Lake City: Bookcraft, 1964), 509.

10. Smith, *Teachings of the Prophet Joseph Smith,* 92–93.

11. Woodruff, in *Journal of Discourses,* 2:200.

12. LeGrand Richards, *Israel! Do You Know?* (Salt Lake City: Deseret Book, 1954), 197.

13. Smith, *History of the Church,* 5:423.

14. Smith, *Teachings of the Prophet Joseph Smith,* 308.

15. Smith, *History of the Church,* 5:337.
16. Smith, *History of the Church,* 6:253.
17. In Lundwall, *Temples of the Most High,* 220.
18. Woodruff, in *Journal of Discourses,* 15:277–78.
19. Smith, *History of the Church,* 1:315.
20. Smith, *History of the Church,* 2:254, 261–62.
21. Joseph Fielding Smith, *Improvement Era,* July 1919, 815–16.
22. Cowley, *Wilford Woodruff,* 509–10.
23. Smith, *History of the Church,* 4:609–10.

APPENDIX

Frequency of the Term *House of Israel* in the Scriptures - 280

Old Testament - 146

Exodus - 2 (16:31; 40:38)
Leviticus - 5 (10:6; 17:3, 8, 10; 22:18)
Numbers - 1 (20:29)
Joshua - 1 (21:45)
Ruth - 1 (4:11)
1 Samuel - 2 (7:2, 3)
2 Samuel - 5 (1:12; 6:5, 15; 12:8; 16:3)
1 Kings - 2 (12:21; 20:31)
Psalms - 3 (98:3; 115:12; 135:19)
Isaiah - 4 (5:7; 14:2; 46:3; 63:7)
Jeremiah - 20 (2:4, 26; 3:18, 20; 5:11, 15; 9:26; 10:1; 11:10, 17; 13:11; 18:6 [2]; 23:8; 31:27, 31, 33; 33:14, 17; 48:13)
Ezekiel - 83 (3:1, 4, 5, 7 [2], 17; 4:3, 4, 5; 5:4; 6:11; 8:6, 10, 11, 12; 9:9; 11:5, 15; 12:6, 9, 10, 24, 27; 13:5, 9; 14:4, 5, 6, 7, 11; 17:2; 18:6, 15, 25, 29 [2], 30, 31; 20:13, 27, 30, 31, 39, 40, 44; 22:18; 24:21; 28:24, 25; 29:6, 16, 21; 33:7, 10, 11, 20; 34:30; 35:15; 36:10, 17, 21, 22 [2], 32, 37; 37:11, 16; 39:12, 22, 23, 25, 29; 40:4; 43:7, 10; 44: 6 [2], 12, 22; 45:6, 8, 17 [2])
Hosea - 5 (1:4, 6; 5:1; 6:10; 11:12)
Amos - 8 (5:1, 3, 4, 25; 6:1, 14; 7:10; 9:9)
Micah - 3 (1:5; 3:1, 9)
Zechariah - 1 (8:13)

New Testament - 6

Matthew - 2 (10:6; 15:24)
Acts - 2 (2:36; 7:42)
Hebrews - 2 (8:8, 10)

Book of Mormon - 122

Title Page - 2 (1st paragraph; 2d paragraph)
1 Nephi - 39 (10:12, 14 [2]; 11:35; 12:9; 13:23 [2], 33, 34; 14:2 [2], 5, 8, 17, 26; 15:12 [3], 14, 16, 17, 18, 20; 19:10, 11, 16, 19, 24 [2]; 21:1 [2], 12, 15; 22:3, 6, 7, 9, 11, 14)
2 Nephi - 23 (3:5, 9, 13, 24; 6:5 [3]; 7:2, 4; 9:1, 53; 10:18, 22; 15:7; 24:2; 25:4; 28:2; 29:1, 2, 12, 14 [2]; 33:13)
Jacob - 5 (5:1, 2, 3; 6:1, 4)
3 Nephi - 36 (10:4, 5 [2], 6, 7; 15:15; 16:5, 7, 8 [2], 9 [2], 11, 12 [2], 13, 14, 15 [2]; 17:14; 20:10, 12, 21, 25, 27; 21:1, 4, 6, 7, 20, 23; 23:2; 29:3, 8, 9; 30:2)
Mormon - 11 (3:17; 4:12; 5:10, 11, 14, 20; 7:1, 2; 8:21 [2]; 9:37)
Ether - 5 (4:14, 15; 13:5 [2], 10)
Moroni - 1 (10:31)

Doctrine and Covenants - 6

14:10; 18:6; 29:12; 39:11; 42:39; 138:25

Pearl of Great Price - 0

Frequency of the Terms *Tribes of Israel, Tribes of the Children of Israel,* or *Tribes of the House of Israel* in the Scriptures - 77

Old Testament - 60

Genesis - 2 (49:16, 28)
Exodus - 3 (24:4; 28:21; 39:14)
Numbers - 4 (31:4; 32:28 "tribes of the children of Israel"; 36:3, 9 "tribes of the children of Israel")
Deuteronomy - 2 (29:21; 33:5)
Joshua - 9 (3:12; 4:5, 8 "tribes of the children of Israel"; 12:7; 14:1 "tribes of the children of Israel"; 19:51 "tribes of the children of Israel"; 21:1 "tribes of the children of Israel"; 22:14; 24:1)
Judges - 7 (18:1; 20:2, 10, 12; 21:5, 8, 15)
1 Samuel - 4 (2:28; 9:21; 10:20; 15:17)

2 Samuel - 7 (5:1; 7:7; 15:2, 10; 19:9; 20:14; 24:2)
1 Kings - 3 (8:16; 11:32; 14:21)
2 Kings - 1 (21:7)
1 Chronicles - 3 (27:16, 22; 29:6)
2 Chronicles - 4 (6:5; 11:16; 12:13; 33:7)
Ezra - 1 (6:17)
Psalms - 1 (78:55)
Ezekiel - 7 (37:19; 47:13, 21, 22; 48:19, 29, 31)
Hosea - 1 (5:9)
Zechariah - 1 (9:1)

New Testament - 4

Matthew - 1 (19:28)
Luke - 1 (22:30)
Revelation - 2 (7:4 "tribes of the children of Israel"; 21:12 "the twelve tribes of the children of Israel")

Book of Mormon - 8

"Tribes of Israel" - 6 (1 Nephi 12:9; 2 Nephi 29:13 [2]; 3 Nephi 17:4; 28:29; Mormon 3:18)
"Tribes of the House of Israel" - 2 (2 Nephi 29:12; 3 Nephi 15:15)

Doctrine and Covenants - 5

"Tribes of Israel" - 5 (77:9 [2], 11, 14; 133:34)

Pearl of Great Price - 1

Article of Faith 10: "restoration of the Ten Tribes"

CHAPTER THREE

THE POWER AND THE PURPOSE OF THE WRITTEN RECORD

ROBERT J. MATTHEWS

I am honored to participate in this twenty-fourth annual Sidney B. Sperry Symposium, especially because it commemorates the one-hundredth anniversary of Brother Sperry's birth.

My topic is the purpose of the Book of Mormon as a written, tangible record. I have a spiritual witness in my soul that the Book of Mormon is a true record and a faithful testament that Jesus Christ is the literal Son of God and our only Redeemer. I will not attempt to prove that the Book of Mormon is true, either by literary or by archaeological evidences, but I will endeavor to explore the significance and usefulness of having a written document such as the Book of Mormon.

A written document is something like a container of canned peaches. Writing preserves the thought and the content and makes it available long after it would otherwise be lost and even forgotten. How enjoyable in January to feast on the harvest of the previous August. And how fortunate in the twentieth century to be spiritually

Robert J. Matthews is professor emeritus of ancient scripture and former dean of Religious Education at Brigham Young University.

fed by the doctrinal discourses of the Savior and the prophets of centuries ago.

But comparison with food is not the best example. I think that comparing the written word to the recording of a complex musical production by a philharmonic orchestra would be a better one. Food is eaten once and is gone, whereas the audio recording of a musical composition can be listened to and analyzed again and again. With music we often do not really "hear" some of the subtle refrains and variations until we have listened several times. Then we wonder why we did not perceive them the first time. Such experience would not be possible if we were restricted to a single exposure—or no exposure at all if we weren't present at the original occasion. Because none of us were even close to any of the happenings of the Book of Mormon, the whole of it would be totally lost to us without a record. As it is with music, so it is with a complex record like the Book of Mormon: in addition to the main thrust of the story, there are subtle connections, relationships, and supporting themes that go unnoticed until it is carefully studied, and it could not be carefully studied if it were not written or recorded in some manner. In a sense, a record makes time stand still, or at least bridges the gap of time between then and now and preserves the event for future generations.

A certain amount of concealed treasure is characteristic of scripture, as Elder Orson Pratt observed from reading a revelation written by Joseph Smith: "These words were given to him, and they contain information and knowledge . . . expressed so simply that a common mind can, in some degree, grasp it, and yet so sublime and so great that when we come to investigate its depths, it requires greater powers and greater understanding than what man naturally possesses."[1] Although Elder Pratt was speaking specifically of Doctrine and

Covenants 88, that same depth is true of revelation generally and hence is true of the Book of Mormon.

The Book of Mormon is a marvelous book, and so is the miraculous nature of its production—including such unusual things as the ministry of the angel Moroni; the use of the Urim and Thummim; the sizeable collection of gold plates with ancient engravings; three mortal witnesses who saw the angel, the plates, and other ancient sacred objects; and the voice of God testifying that the book is true. All these things add to the mystique and the wonderment of it.

To explore the purpose of the Book of Mormon as a written record, we shall examine, first, what the Lord has declared to be the purpose and mission of the Book of Mormon as recorded in the Doctrine and Covenants; second, what the Prophet Joseph Smith said about the Book of Mormon; and third, what the Book of Mormon says about itself and its purpose.

WHAT THE LORD HAS DECLARED ABOUT THE BOOK OF MORMON

In the beginning of this dispensation the Lord Jesus Christ frequently stated just what the Book of Mormon is and what he intends to accomplish by it:

> And after having received the record of the Nephites, yea, even my servant Joseph Smith, Jun., might have power to translate through the mercy of God, by the power of God, the Book of Mormon. (D&C 1:29)

> Behold, thou art Joseph, and thou wast chosen to do the work of the Lord, but because of transgression, if thou art not aware thou wilt fall. . . .
>
> And when thou deliveredst up that which God had given thee sight and power to translate, thou deliveredst up that which was sacred into the hands of a wicked man. . . .

Nevertheless, my work shall go forth, for inasmuch as the knowledge of a Savior has come unto the world, through the testimony of the Jews, even so shall the knowledge of a Savior come unto my people—

And to the Nephites, and the Jacobites, and the Josephites, and the Zoramites, through the testimony of their fathers—

And this testimony shall come to the knowledge of the Lamanites, and the Lemuelites, and the Ishmaelites, who dwindled in unbelief because of the iniquity of their fathers, whom the Lord has suffered to destroy their brethren the Nephites, because of their iniquities and their abominations.

And for this very purpose are these plates preserved, which contain these records—that the promises of the Lord might be fulfilled, which he made to his people;

And that the Lamanites might come to the knowledge of their fathers, and that they might know the promises of the Lord, and that they may believe the gospel and rely upon the merits of Jesus Christ, and be glorified through faith in his name, and that through their repentance they might be saved. Amen. [D&C 3:9, 12, 16–20]

For hereafter you shall be ordained and go forth and deliver my words unto the children of men.

Behold, if they will not believe my words, they would not believe you, my servant Joseph, if it were possible that you should show them all these things which I have committed unto you.

Oh, this unbelieving and stiffnecked generation—mine anger is kindled against them.

Behold, verily I say unto you, I have reserved those things which I have entrusted unto you, my servant Joseph, for a wise purpose in me, and it shall be made known unto future generations;

But this generation shall have my word through you;

And in addition to your testimony, the testimony

of three of my servants, whom I shall call and ordain, unto whom I will show these things, and they shall go forth with my words that are given through you.

Yea, they shall know of a surety that these things are true, for from heaven will I declare it unto them. [D&C 5:6–12]

Behold, I am Jesus Christ, the Son of God. . . .

I am he who said—Other sheep have I which are not of this fold—unto my disciples, and many there were that understood me not.

And I will show unto this people that I had other sheep, and that they were a branch of the house of Jacob;

And I will bring to light their marvelous works, which they did in my name;

Yea, and I will also bring to light my gospel which was ministered unto them, and, behold, they shall not deny that which you have received, but they shall build it up, and shall bring to light the true points of my doctrine, yea, and the only doctrine which is in me.

And this I do that I may establish my gospel, that there may not be so much contention. [D&C 10:57–63]

And again, I command thee [Martin Harris] that thou shalt not covet thine own property, but impart it freely to the printing of the Book of Mormon, which contains the truth and the word of God—

Which is my word to the Gentile, that soon it may go to the Jew, of whom the Lamanites are a remnant, that they may believe the gospel, and look not for a Messiah to come who has already come. [D&C 19:26–27]

And gave him [Joseph Smith] power from on high, by the means which were before prepared, to translate the Book of Mormon;

Which contains a record of a fallen people, and the

fulness of the gospel of Jesus Christ to the Gentiles and to the Jews also;

Which was given by inspiration, and is confirmed to others by the ministering of angels, and is declared unto the world by them—

Proving to the world that the holy scriptures are true, and that God does inspire men and call them to his holy work in this age and generation, as well as in generations of old;

Thereby showing that he is the same God yesterday, today, and forever. Amen.

Therefore, having so great witnesses, by them shall the world be judged, even as many as shall hereafter come to a knowledge of this work. [D&C 20:8–13]

And your minds in times past have been darkened because of unbelief, and because you have treated lightly the things you have received—

Which vanity and unbelief have brought the whole church under condemnation.

And this condemnation resteth upon the children of Zion, even all.

And they shall remain under this condemnation until they repent and remember the new covenant, even the Book of Mormon and the former commandments which I have given them, not only to say, but to do according to that which I have written. [D&C 84:54–57]

And again, verily I say unto you, let no man pay stock to the quorum of the Nauvoo House unless he shall be a believer in the Book of Mormon, and the revelations I have given unto you, saith the Lord your God. [D&C 124:119]

The Lord has clearly stated the following fundamentals about why he has brought forth the Book of Mormon, a plan that has been in operation on earth for more than forty centuries, all the way back to the tower of Babel.

1. Joseph Smith was chosen and was given sight and power and mercy from God to translate the Book of Mormon (see D&C 1:29; 3:9).

2. The manuscript containing the translation was sacred (see D&C 3:12; 20:6–8).

3. The Lord calls the Book of Mormon "my work" and declares that it contains the knowledge of the Savior and is directed to the latter-day Nephites and Lamanites because it is a message from their own fathers (see D&C 3:16–18).

4. The Book of Mormon is a separate and a second witness, along with the Bible, that Jesus is the Savior (see D&C 3:16).

5. The gold plates have been preserved for the very purpose of fulfilling the Lord's promise to ancient prophets that he would bring a knowledge of the Savior to the latter-day descendants of the Nephites and Lamanites from their own fathers (see D&C 3:19–20).

6. The record is designed to teach the Lamanites about their fathers and about the promises of the Lord, and bring them to faith, repentance, and salvation through the merits of Christ (see D&C 3:20).

7. Those who will not believe the testimony of Joseph Smith would not believe that the Book of Mormon is from God, even if Joseph Smith showed them the plates and other sacred objects (see D&C 5:7–8).

8. Three witnesses besides Joseph Smith shall testify that they have seen the sacred objects, and also that God declared the truth of it to them by his own voice from heaven (see D&C 5:11–12).

9. The Book of Mormon is a record of the "other sheep" spoken of by Jesus in the Bible and contains an account of "marvelous works" that those people did in the name of the Lord (see D&C 10:59–61).

10. There will be people who will accept and believe

the Book of Mormon when they hear it and shall bring to light the true points of doctrine it contains (see D&C 10:62–63).

11. The Book of Mormon is the truth and the word of God to the Gentiles, to the Jews, and to the Lamanites to convince them that Jesus is the true Messiah (see D&C 19:26–27).

12. The Book of Mormon is a record of a fallen people and contains the fulness of the gospel of Jesus Christ to the Gentiles and to the Jews (see D&C 20:9).

13. The truth of the Book of Mormon is confirmed by the ministry of angels, and it also proves that the holy scriptures (the Bible) are true and that God still calls people to his holy work (see D&C 20:10–12).

14. The Book of Mormon proves that God is the same yesterday, today, and forever (see D&C 20:12).

15. The world will be judged by the knowledge that is in the holy scriptures, both the Bible and the Book of Mormon (see D&C 20:13).

16. Because of unbelief and neglect of the Book of Mormon and the other revelations, the whole Church has been under a condemnation that can only be removed by repentance and attention to the teachings of the Book of Mormon (see D&C 84:54–57).

17. Only believers in the Book of Mormon were to be allowed to contribute money to the building of the Nauvoo House (see D&C 124:119–20).

It is obvious that the purposes of the Lord could not be fulfilled if the Book of Mormon were not available as a written document, produced in multiple copies, and made available to many people in a language and form they could read and understand. The Book of Mormon has a mission not only to inform but also to convince. The Lord wants the Book of Mormon written, translated, distributed, read, and obeyed.

WHAT THE PROPHET JOSEPH SMITH SAID ABOUT THE BOOK OF MORMON

From among the many statements by Joseph Smith about the Book of Mormon, I have selected three that illustrate how he valued its content. The first was said on 21 April 1834 to a conference of elders in which the Prophet's central theme was the necessity of latter-day revelation:

> We are differently situated from any other people that ever existed upon this earth; consequently those former revelations [i.e., the Bible] cannot be suited to our conditions; they were given to other people, who were before us; [Therefore]—Take away the Book of Mormon and the revelations, and where is our religion? We have none; for without Zion, and a place of deliverance, we must fall.[2]

The second was written 19 October 1840 in an epistle from the Prophet in Nauvoo, Illinois, to the Quorum of the Twelve in Great Britain:

> I am informed that the Book of Mormon is likewise printed [in England], which I am glad to hear, and should be pleased to hear that it was printed in all the different languages of the earth.[3]

The third was spoken to the Twelve Apostles on 28 November 1841 in Nauvoo and written by the Prophet in his journal:

> I told the brethren that the Book of Mormon was the most correct of any book on earth, and the keystone of our religion, and a man would get nearer to God by abiding by its precepts, than by any other book.[4]

WHAT THE BOOK OF MORMON SAYS ABOUT ITSELF

Passages within the Book of Mormon that relate to the need for the written word are so numerous that only those having a direct bearing on the value of such a record will be discussed here. The Book of Mormon is emphatic that the Lord would use a tangible document containing not only historical fact but also points of doctrine to accomplish his work on the earth in the last days. The written word forms a base and a standard.

The Book of Mormon title page, which seems to have been written by Moroni, or maybe partly by Mormon and partly by Moroni,[5] presents so much information in so few words that we quote it in full:

> THE
> BOOK OF MORMON
> AN ACCOUNT WRITTEN BY
> THE HAND OF MORMON
> UPON PLATES
> TAKEN FROM THE PLATES OF NEPHI
>
> Wherefore, it is an abridgment of the record of the people of Nephi, and also of the Lamanites—Written to the Lamanites, who are a remnant of the house of Israel; and also to Jew and Gentile—Written by way of commandment, and also by the spirit of prophecy and of revelation—Written and sealed up, and hid up unto the Lord, that they might not be destroyed—To come forth by the gift and power of God unto the interpretation thereof—Sealed by the hand of Moroni, and hid up unto the Lord, to come forth in due time by way of the Gentile—The interpretation thereof by the gift of God.
>
> An abridgment taken from the Book of Ether also, which is a record of the people of Jared, who were scattered at the time the Lord confounded the language of the people, when they were building a tower to get to heaven—Which is to show unto the remnant of the House of Israel what great things the Lord hath done for their fathers; and that they may know the covenants of the Lord, that they are not cast off forever—And also to the convincing of the Jew and

> Gentile that JESUS is the CHRIST, the ETERNAL GOD, manifesting himself unto all nations—And now, if there are faults they are the mistakes of men; wherefore, condemn not the things of God, that ye may be found spotless at the judgment-seat of Christ.

The title page is particularly important to us because it states directly the intent and purpose of the Book of Mormon:

1. Written to Lamanite, Jew, and Gentile
2. By the command of the Lord
3. By revelation and the spirit of prophecy
4. To come forth by miraculous means, through the gift and power of God
5. To show to the house of Israel what great things the Lord has done for their fathers
6. That the covenants of the Lord might be known
7. To the convincing of Jew and Gentile that Jesus is the Christ, the Eternal God, manifesting himself to all nations

We will now examine several of these topics individually, for if they are mentioned on the title page, they must also have been given attention within the book itself. In fact, in the Book of Mormon these concepts overlap considerably and are not generally spoken of separately. That presents no real problem because it actually reemphasizes and reinforces the words of each prophet and shows also that each of these topics is related to the others and that each would be incomplete by itself. All are germane to the purpose of the book.

Written to Lamanite, Jew, and Gentile

To the Lamanites

Near the close of his life, Mormon, the chief writer and compiler of the book, writes to future generations of his people—primarily to the Lamanites of the latter days:

> Know ye that ye are of the house of Israel.
>
> Know ye that ye must come unto repentance, or ye cannot be saved. . . .
>
> Know ye that ye must come to the knowledge of your fathers, and repent of all your sins and iniquities, and believe in Jesus Christ, that he is the Son of God, and that he was slain by the Jews, and by the power of the Father he hath risen again, whereby he hath gained the victory over the grave; and also in him is the sting of death swallowed up. . . .
>
> Therefore repent, and be baptized in the name of Jesus, and lay hold upon the gospel of Christ, which shall be set before you, not only in this record but also in the record which shall come unto the Gentiles from the Jews, which record shall come from the Gentiles unto you. [Mormon 7:2–3, 5, 8]

To the Jews

Nephi wrote that the Jews would be scattered among all nations and remain scattered until they begin to believe in the atonement of the Son of God. He said that in the due time of the Lord the Nephite record will be presented to them to convince them that Jesus is that true Messiah and Son of God:

> Wherefore, the Jews shall be scattered among all nations . . . .
>
> And the Lord will set his hand again the second time to restore his people from their lost and fallen state. Wherefore, he will proceed to do a marvelous work and a wonder among the children of men.
>
> Wherefore, he shall bring forth his words unto them, which words shall judge them at the last day, for they shall be given them for the purpose of convincing them of the true Messiah, who was rejected by them; and unto the convincing of them that they

> need not look forward any more for a Messiah to come, for there should not any come, save it should be a false Messiah which should deceive the people; for there is save one Messiah spoken of by the prophets, and that Messiah is he who should be rejected of the Jews. . . .
>
> Wherefore for this cause hath the Lord God promised unto me that these things which I write shall be kept and preserved, and handed down unto my seed. . . .
>
> Wherefore, these things shall go from generation to generation as long as the earth shall stand; and they shall go according to the will and pleasure of God; and the nations who shall possess them shall be judged of them according to the words which are written. [2 Nephi 25:15, 17–18, 21–22]

Nephi continued:

> And now, my beloved brethren, and also Jew, and all ye ends of the earth, hearken unto these words and believe in Christ. [2 Nephi 33:10]

The prophet Mormon also wrote concerning the Jews:

> And this is the commandment which I have received; [that my writings] shall come forth according to the commandment of the Lord, when he shall see fit, in his wisdom.
>
> And behold, they shall go unto the unbelieving of the Jews; and for this intent shall they go—that they may be persuaded that Jesus is the Christ, the Son of the living God; that the Father may bring about, through his most Beloved, his great and eternal purpose, in restoring the Jews, or all the house of Israel, to the land of their inheritance, which the Lord their God hath given them, unto the fulfilling of his covenant. [Mormon 5:13–14]

To the Gentiles

Nephi said:

> And as I spake concerning the convincing of the Jews, that Jesus is the very Christ, it must needs be that the Gentiles be convinced also that Jesus is the Christ, the Eternal God. [2 Nephi 26:12]

Nearly a thousand years later, the prophet Mormon also wrote directly to the Gentiles of the latter days:

> Hearken, O ye Gentiles, and hear the words of Jesus Christ, the Son of the living God, which he hath commanded me that I should speak concerning you, for, behold he commandeth me that I should write, saying:
>
> Turn, all ye Gentiles, from your wicked ways; and repent of your evil doings, of your lyings and deceivings, and of your whoredoms, and of your secret abominations, and your idolatries, and of your murders, and your priestcrafts , and your envyings, and your strifes, and from all your wickedness and abominations, and come unto me, and be baptized in my name, that ye may receive a remission of your sins, and be filled with the Holy Ghost, that ye may be numbered with my people who are of the house of Israel. [3 Nephi 30:1–2]

And still later Moroni wrote these words of warning directly to the Gentiles who would occupy the western hemisphere:

> And this cometh unto you, O ye Gentiles, that ye may know the decrees of God—that ye may repent, and not continue in your iniquities until the fulness come, that ye may not bring down the fulness of the wrath of God upon you as the inhabitants of the land have hitherto done.
>
> Behold, this is a choice land, and whatsoever nation shall possess it shall be free from bondage, and from

> captivity, and from all other nations under heaven, if they will but serve the God of the land, who is Jesus Christ, who hath been manifested by the things which we have written. [Ether 2:11–12]

By the Command of the Lord, by Revelation and the Spirit of Prophecy, through the Gift and Power of God

To convince all these peoples that Jesus is the true Messiah, the Lord designed that a new book should come forth to corroborate the truth of the Bible and also to testify afresh, or be a second witness, that Jesus is the Christ. That new book is the Book of Mormon, which is spoken of in 2 Nephi 27 as a "sealed" book. Nephi said concerning it:

> And the things which shall be written out of the book shall be of great worth unto the children of men, and especially unto our seed, which is a remnant of the house of Israel. [2 Nephi 28:2]

Nephi continued:

> And now, I would prophesy somewhat more concerning the Jews and the Gentiles. For after the book of which I have spoken shall come forth, and be written unto the Gentiles, and sealed up again unto the Lord, there shall be many which shall believe the words which are written; and they shall carry them forth unto the remnant of our seed.
>
> And then shall the remnant of our seed know concerning us, how that we came out from Jerusalem, and that they are descendants of the Jews.
>
> And the gospel of Jesus Christ shall be declared among them; wherefore, they shall be restored unto the knowledge of their fathers, and also to the knowledge of Jesus Christ, which was had among their fathers.
>
> And then shall they rejoice; for they shall know

> that it is a blessing unto them from the hand of God. [2 Nephi 30:3–6]

Why bring about a new book when the world has the Bible already? For one thing, the Book of Mormon is a second witness to the work of God. The Lord said that "the testimony of two nations is a witness that I am God, that I remember one nation like unto another. Wherefore I speak the same words to one nation, like unto another" (2 Nephi 29:8).

The Bible has been available to the world for thousands of years; however, the originals are gone, and copies have been altered by men, so that though the message of the Bible is still true, it is incomplete and lacks the necessary directions it once contained. On the other hand, the plates of the Book of Mormon, having been buried in the ground out of reach of humans, have not been altered. Therefore the Book of Mormon is still pure and "original" and makes known many of the covenants of the Lord that have been lost from the Bible (see 1 Nephi 13:20–29, 35–41). As the prophet Mormon said:

> For behold, this [Book of Mormon] is written for the intent that ye may believe that [Bible]; and if ye believe that ye will believe this also; and if ye believe this ye will know concerning your fathers, and also the marvelous works which were wrought by the power of God among them. [Mormon 7:9]

The Great Things the Lord Has Done for the Fathers

The Book of Mormon prophets exhibit a keen interest in the family. This is seen in four areas. First are the frequent declarations that the people are of the house of Israel and particularly of Joseph. Second, there is repeated reference to the blessings and mercies of God that were given to their fathers (Book of Mormon prophets never speak of ancestors or progenitors; it is always the "fathers"). Third, the prophets are deeply concerned for the spiritual well-being of their immediate families, especially their children, and also their brethren the Lamanites. Fourth, concern is repeatedly expressed for the spiritual welfare of their descendants, even thousands of years in the future.

The constant emphasis on being literally of the house of Israel, and of Joseph, is on account of the covenants that the Lord made with Abraham, Isaac, Jacob, and Joseph regarding their families. Although these promises are valid in every generation, they will reach fruition and fulfillment in the latter days. When Jesus visited the Nephites, he repeatedly reminded them that they were "the children of the prophets" and "of the covenant" of Abraham (3 Nephi 20:25) and of the lineage of Joseph (see 3 Nephi 15:12–13).

The Lord commanded the prophets to write the Book of Mormon as an instrument of restoration. It is a special tool of the Lord in fulfilling his ancient promises to the fathers that he would remember their children. Among the "great things" and "marvelous works" recorded in the Book of Mormon that the Lord has done for the "fathers" are the following:

1. He brought Lehi, Ishmael, and their families out of Jerusalem and thus spared them the destruction that soon came upon Jerusalem (see 1 Nephi 1–8).

2. He preserved Lehi's party in the wilderness and on the sea, and he brought them safely to the promised land of the Western Hemisphere. He gave them food, the Liahona, and the comfort of the Holy Ghost (see 1 Nephi 9–17).

3. He taught the Nephites the gospel by visions, the ministry of angels, and the Holy Ghost, and made promises and eternal covenants with them concerning

their own lives and also their posterity (see 1 Nephi 8, 11–14; 2 Nephi 1–3; Alma 9:20–23).

4. He eased the heavy burdens of those in bondage (see Mosiah 24:8–15).

5. He freed such groups as Alma and his people from physical captivity (see Mosiah 24:17–25) and also from the bondage of sin in giving them freedom and also remission of sins. As Alma said, God "delivered their souls from hell" and changed their hearts (Alma 5:4–7).

6. He blessed the prophets in their ministries, sometimes freeing them from prison, providing food, and giving them joy and success in their labors even in affliction (see Alma 14:17–29).

7. Jesus personally visited the people several times after his resurrection and taught them, healed the sick, and blessed the children. Above all, he proved to them that he was the God of Israel, had been slain for the sins of the world, and had truly risen from the dead with a tangible body (see 3 Nephi 11–28).

We cannot miss the fact that one reason the Lord wanted a record kept and the Book of Mormon produced is so that in the latter days mankind would know of his great works among the people in ancient America. That truth is further established in the following passages:

> The voice of the Lord came to [the people of Alma] in their afflictions, saying: Lift up your heads and be of good comfort, for I know of the covenant which ye have made unto me; and I will covenant with my people and deliver them out of bondage.
>
> And I will also ease the burdens which are put upon your shoulders, that even you cannot feel them upon your backs, even while you are in bondage; and this will I do that ye may stand as witnesses for me hereafter, and that ye may know of a surety that I, the Lord God, do visit my people in their afflictions.

> And now it came to pass that the burdens which were laid upon Alma and his brethren were made light; yea, the Lord did strengthen them that they could bear up their burdens with ease, and they did submit cheerfully and with patience to all the will of the Lord. . . .
>
> Yea, and in the valley of Alma they poured out their thanks to God because he had been merciful unto them, and eased their burdens, and had delivered them out of bondage; for they were in bondage, and none could deliver them except it were the Lord their God.
>
> And they gave thanks to God, yea, all their men and all their women and all their children that could speak lifted their voices in the praises of their God. (Mosiah 24:13–15, 21–22)

These people do in effect "stand as witnesses" again and again every time anyone reads these words that have been written about them.

More than four hundred years after the time of Alma, the prophet Moroni spoke of the mercies of the Lord not only to the ancient Nephites but to the whole family of the earth:

> Behold, I would exhort you that when ye shall read these things, if it be wisdom in God that ye should read them, that ye would remember how merciful the Lord hath been unto the children of men, from the creation of Adam even down until the time that ye shall receive these things, and ponder it in your hearts. [Moroni 10:3]

Some passages illustrate both the immediate and the long-range concerns the Nephite prophets had for the family. From Nephi we read:

> And we talk of Christ, we rejoice in Christ, we preach of Christ, we prophesy of Christ, and we write

> according to our prophecies, that our children may know to what source they may look for a remission of their sins. [2 Nephi 25:26]

From Jacob:

> Now behold, it came to pass that I, Jacob, having ministered much unto my people in word, (and I cannot write but a little of my words, because of the difficulty of engraving our words upon plates) and we know that the things which we write upon the plates must remain;
>
> But whatsoever things we write upon anything save it be upon plates must perish and vanish away; but we can write a few words upon plates, which will give our children, and also our beloved brethren, a small degree of knowledge concerning us, or concerning their fathers—
>
> Now in this thing we do rejoice; and we labor diligently to engraven these words upon plates, hoping that our beloved brethren and our children will receive them with thankful hearts, and look upon them that they may learn with joy and not with sorrow, neither with contempt, concerning their first parents. [Jacob 4:1–3]

It is clear that Jacob had his mind focused on readers who would live in future generations, hence his desire to write on such durable material as metal.

Because the prophet Enos was concerned about the unbelief and wickedness of the Lamanites, he asked the Lord in mighty prayer to preserve the Nephite records for future use among the Lamanites. Enos's words are as follows:

> And I had faith, and I did cry unto God that he would preserve the records; and he covenanted with me that he would bring them forth unto the Lamanites in his own due time.

> And I, Enos, knew it would be according to the covenant which he had made; wherefore my soul did rest.
>
> And the Lord said unto me: Thy fathers have also required of me this thing; and it shall be done unto them according to their faith; for their faith was like unto thine. [Enos 1:16–18]

The "fathers" in this case include Enos's own father Jacob, his uncle Nephi, his grandfather Lehi, and perhaps also such prophets as Zenos and Zenock, who were of the lineage of Joseph but who lived much earlier than Lehi and yet knew of Lehi and his posterity (see 3 Nephi 10:16).

That the Covenants of the Lord Might Be Known

The particular advantage of having the scriptures in writing is stated plainly by King Benjamin, who diligently nurtured and cared for his sons:

> And he also taught them concerning the records which were engraven on the plates of brass, saying: My sons, I would that ye should remember that were it not for these plates, which contain these records and these commandments, we must have suffered in ignorance, even at this present time, not knowing the mysteries of God.
>
> For it were not possible that our father, Lehi, could have remembered all these things, to have taught them to his children, except it were for the help of these plates; for he having been taught in the language of the Egyptians therefore he could read these engravings, and teach them to his children, that thereby they could teach them to their children, and so fulfilling the commandments of God, even down to this present time.
>
> I say unto you, my sons, were it not for these things, which have been kept and preserved by the hand of God, that we might read and understand of

> his mysteries, and have his commandments always before our eyes, that even our fathers would have dwindled in unbelief, and we should have been like unto our brethren, the Lamanites, who know nothing concerning these things, or even do not believe them when they are taught them, because of the traditions of their fathers, which are not correct.
>
> O my sons, I would that ye should remember that these sayings are true, and also that these records are true. And behold, also the plates of Nephi, which contain the records and the sayings of our fathers from the time they left Jerusalem until now, and they are true; and we can know of their surety because we have them before our eyes. [Mosiah 1:3–6]

Although the foregoing was written about the plates of brass, the sentiments apply just as pointedly to the Book of Mormon.

Alma taught his son Helaman that the written scriptures "have enlarged the memory of this people, yea, and convinced many of the error of their ways, and brought them to the knowledge of their God" (Alma 37:8).

He further explained that missionaries are more likely to be successful when they carry with them the tangible, written word of the Lord: "Yea, I say unto you, were it not for these things that these records do contain, which are on these plates, Ammon and his brethren could not have convinced so many thousands of the Lamanites of the incorrect tradition of their fathers; yea, these records and their words brought them unto repentance; that is, they brought them to the knowledge of the Lord their God, and to rejoice in Jesus Christ their Redeemer" (Alma 37:9).

Convincing Jew and Gentile That Jesus Is the Christ

Convincing Jew and Gentile that Jesus is the Christ can hardly be a separate category because all of the previous categories have also dealt directly with this subject. All other subjects are contributory to the knowledge that Jesus is the true and only Messiah for the whole earth. The Book of Mormon lists nearly 100 separate names and titles for Jesus and contains direct reference to the Savior at least 3,471 times. Of the 239 chapters in the Book of Mormon, only six do not speak directly of the Savior: Mosiah 9, 22; Alma 51–52; and Helaman 1–2, which deal primarily with political government and war. The Book of Mormon not only tells who Jesus is as a person and as a God but it also explains better than any other book how the Atonement works in the lives of human beings—and that not just by doctrinal precept and discourse but by its demonstration in the lives of Lehi, Nephi, Alma, Amulek, Lamoni, and many others whose lives were changed by the power of Jesus Christ.

But what makes the Book of Mormon convincing? Its purpose is not only to inform but to convince the reader that Jesus is the Christ. The strongest factor is that the book is true, and being the Lord's doing, his Spirit bears witness to the reader who sincerely desires to know and who prays with real intent concerning it.

A second factor is that the Book of Mormon is not an intellectual treatise. It does not attempt to win advocates by logic or reason. The Book of Mormon is testimony from those who experienced the things of the soul. It speaks to the heart and the spirit.

A third factor is that the Book of Mormon uses a great many colorful, expressive, dynamic, action-packed, and emotionally charged words (see Job 6:25).

And fourth, doctrinal points are often made clear by contrasts and opposites. The following passages exemplify these traits.

King Benjamin gave this thought:

> Therefore if that man repenteth not, and remaineth

> and dieth an enemy to God, the demands of divine justice do awaken his immortal soul to a lively sense of his own guilt, which doth cause him to shrink from the presence of the Lord, and doth fill his breast with guilt, and pain, and anguish, which is like an unquenchable fire, whose flame ascendeth up forever and ever.
>
> And now I say unto you, that mercy hath no claim on that man; therefore his final doom is to endure a never-ending torment. [Mosiah 2:38–39]

Then King Benjamin made his point even clearer by contrast:

> I have spoken plainly unto you that ye might understand, I pray that ye should awake to a remembrance of the awful situation of those that have fallen into transgression.
>
> And moreover, I would desire that ye should consider on the blessed and happy state of those that keep the commandments of God. For behold, they are blessed in all things, both temporal and spiritual. [Mosiah 2:40–41]

Another example of teaching by contrast occurs in Alma's reflections to his son Helaman in telling of his own conversion, which was initiated by the ministration of an angel:

> But I was racked with eternal torment, for my soul was harrowed up to the greatest degree and racked with all my sins.
>
> Yea, I did remember all my sins and iniquities, for which I was tormented with the pains of hell; yea, I saw that I had rebelled against my God, and that I had not kept his holy commandments. . . . yea, and in fine so great had been my iniquities, that the very thought of coming into the presence of my God did rack my soul with inexpressible horror.
>
> Oh, thought I, that I could be banished and become

> extinct both soul and body, that I might not be brought to stand in the presence of my God, to be judged of my deeds.
>
> And now, for three days and for three nights was I racked, even with the pains of a damned soul.
>
> And it came to pass that as I was thus racked with torment, while I was harrowed up by the memory of my many sins, behold, I remembered also to have heard my father prophesy unto the people concerning the coming of one Jesus Christ, a Son of God, to atone for the sins of the world.
>
> Now, as my mind caught hold upon this thought, I cried within my heart: O Jesus, thou Son of God, have mercy on me, who am in the gall of bitterness, and am encircled about by the everlasting chains of death.
>
> And now, behold, when I thought this, I could remember my pains no more; yea, I was harrowed up by the memory of my sins no more.
>
> And oh, what joy, and what marvelous light I did behold; yea, my soul was filled with joy as exceeding as was my pain!
>
> Yea, I say unto you, my son, that there could be nothing so exquisite and so bitter as were my pains. Yea, and again I say unto you, my son, that on the other hand, there can be nothing so exquisite and sweet as was my joy.
>
> Yea, methought I saw, even as our father Lehi saw, God sitting upon his throne, surrounded with numberless concourses of angels, in the attitude of singing and praising their God; yea, and my soul did long to be there. [Alma 36:12–22]

The prophet Jacob, perhaps the most expressive writer in the Book of Mormon, uses many colorful phrases within a few paragraphs when he speaks of the "all-searching eye" of God; the "chains" of the devil; the "glorious day" of the righteous; and of the "awful fear," "awful misery," and "awful reality" awaiting the unrepentant (2 Nephi 9:44–47).

It was probably such vividness of language that led Elder Orson Pratt to say:

> The nature of the message in the Book of Mormon is such, that if true, no one can possibly be saved and reject it; if false, no one can possibly be saved and receive it.[6]

"FOR A WISE PURPOSE"

As we have noted, the prophets in the Book of Mormon were commanded by the Lord to keep a record of their history, their doctrine, the fulfillment of prophecy, and the blessings they received. And though they knew that they were commanded to write and they knew what to write, they did not know all the reasons why they should write. They did know that their records would be preserved and given to future generations to assist in the Restoration, but some things were spoken of only as being for a wise purpose in the Lord. Nephi makes that observation when he was commanded to keep separate records:

> Wherefore, the Lord hath commanded me to make these plates for a wise purpose in him, which purpose I know not.
>
> But the Lord knoweth all things from the beginning; wherefore, he prepareth a way to accomplish all his works among the children of men; for behold, he hath all power unto the fulfilling of all his words. And thus it is. Amen. [1 Nephi 9:5–6]

Nephi later writes that these records were kept for the instruction of his people, "and also for other wise purposes, which purposes are known unto the Lord" (1 Nephi 19:3). Mormon speaks of assembling his record for "a wise purpose" manifested by the Spirit of the Lord.

Though Mormon explains that he himself does not know everything about what the purpose will be, yet he is confident that "the Lord knoweth all things which are to come" (Words of Mormon 1:6–7). Alma taught his son Helaman that continuing to write the record was for a "wise purpose" (Alma 37:2). He tells Helaman that sacred records, including the plates of brass, have been kept and preserved for a "wise purpose" known only to God (Alma 37:12), and by this method God would "show forth his power unto future generations" (Alma 37:14, 18). Alma states that one purpose is for missionary work but that there are other purposes (see Alma 37:19–47).

These "wise purposes" are also referred to in Doctrine and Covenants 3:19, 5:9, and 10:34–41. Though there the matter of the lost 116 pages is the principal topic, clearly more is involved, because the words "this shall be made known unto future generations" (D&C 5:9) are used. We do not yet know all that is included in these "wise purposes" and why the Lord wanted the record to contain certain particular things. But definitely it is not limited to the episode of the lost 116 pages.

We know that the Mulekites carried no records with them and as a consequence lost their language and their doctrine (see Omni 1:16–18). And Jesus specifically wanted the prophecy of Samuel the Lamanite to be recorded complete in every detail (see 3 Nephi 23:6–13). Likewise Jesus gave the Nephites the words of Malachi 3 and 4 to be included in their records (see 3 Nephi 24–25). And the plates of brass are to be preserved and eventually go to all nations of the earth (see 1 Nephi 5:18; Alma 37:1–12). These multiple scriptures were not only for that day but for "future generations" (3 Nephi 26:2).

Because the small plates of Nephi were so providentially available and were used to fill the gap caused by the loss of the 116 pages of manuscript, I wonder if we have simply supposed that that one episode is all that was meant by the statement about "wise purposes." I think it was only one of several wise purposes yet to be experienced. What might some others be? They could very well be in the area of textual criticism, and in ancient world history, and in anthropology, and in other social sciences. It is my expectation and anticipation that the Lord will yet bring to light the textual documentary evidence that will prove that the Bible and the Book of Mormon are historically correct and are actual history. Such additional records could show various patterns of revelation that existed anciently, which would substantiate the mission, the translations (such as the Book of Mormon, the Joseph Smith Translation, and the book of Abraham), and the teachings of Joseph Smith in every particular.

When I was about eighteen years old and reading the Book of Mormon for the first time, I felt the Spirit work in me and manifest that it was true. I recall particularly being strongly moved by the statement in 2 Nephi 29:8 that the testimony of two nations was a witness that the Lord is God and that he spoke the same words to one nation like unto another. I felt the truth of it but didn't know why it was important. I have since come to realize the great use that can be made of having an ancient text to compare with present manuscripts of the Bible. I also realize that such a witness is necessary so that the honest in heart and the meek will learn how to find salvation and be justified on the day of judgment, whereas the unbelieving, having the same evidence, will be left without excuse.

NOTES

1. Orson Pratt, 14 Mar. 1875, in N. B. Lundwall, comp., *Wonders of the Universe* (Salt Lake City: N. B. Lundwall, 1937), 197.

2. Joseph Smith, *Teachings of the Prophet Joseph Smith,* sel. Joseph Fielding Smith (Salt Lake City: Deseret Book, 1976), 70–71.

3. Smith, *Teachings of the Prophet Joseph Smith,* 176.

4. Smith, *Teachings of the Prophet Joseph Smith,* 194.

5. In the 1840 and 1852 editions of the Book of Mormon the name Moroni was placed after the second paragraph, suggesting that he was the author of the title page, or at least of that paragraph, but his name has not appeared there in all subsequent printings.

6. "Divine Authenticity of the Book of Mormon," published 15 October 1850, Liverpool, England; in Orson Pratt, *Orson Pratt's Works on the Doctrines of the Gospel* (Salt Lake City: Deseret News Press, 1945), 107.

CHAPTER FOUR

THE REGENERATION OF FALLEN MAN

ROBERT L. MILLET

In a revelation given to the Prophet Joseph Smith, the Book of Mormon is described as "a record of a fallen people" (D&C 20:9). It is certainly a narrative history of the rise and fall of two great civilizations, a sobering chronicle of how pride and secret combinations usher nations into destruction. It is also a reminder that without ever-present divine assistance and the regenerating powers of the atonement of Christ, men and women remain forevermore lost and fallen creatures. "Why is it so vital," Elder William R. Bradford asked, "that we have a record of a fallen people? Why would such a record merit the trial and suffering of those who have sacrificed to bring forth this book, even to the constant and direct intervention of God Almighty?" Elder Bradford then answered his own question: "I submit to you that no one, regardless of race or creed, can ever understand the role of and the need for a savior and a redeemer unless he first knows from what he needs to be saved or redeemed. No person, regardless of his religion or tradition, can understand victory over death and the terms

---

Robert L. Millet is dean of Religious Education at Brigham Young University.

upon which his salvation depends unless he understands the doctrine of fallen man."[1]

Or, as Elder Bradford stated on another occasion, "The Book of Mormon contains the record of a fallen people. It outlines how man got into a condition which subjects him to death and separation from God. The Book of Mormon also contains the fulness of the gospel of Jesus Christ. It outlines for us in perfect clarity what has been done for us and what we must do ourselves to overcome our fallen condition and return to the presence of God. . . . The Book of Mormon holds out to us a fulness of what we must be saved from. It gives us a complete understanding of the role of, and the need for, a savior. It is another testament of Jesus Christ."[2]

The plight and the promise, the malady and the medicine, the Fall and the Atonement—that is the burden of the Book of Mormon.

THE FALL AND ITS EFFECTS

The Latter-day Saint view of the Fall is remarkably optimistic. We believe that Adam and Eve went into the Garden of Eden to fall, that what they did had the approbation of the Gods and thus is termed a transgression and not a sin, and that their fall was as much a part of the foreordained plan of the Father as was the very Atonement. We believe in the words of the Prophet Joseph Smith, that "Adam was made to open the way of the world,"[3] that the Fall was a move downward but forward in the eternal scheme of things, and that it "brought man into the world and set his feet upon progression's highway."[4] We do not believe, as did John Calvin, that men and women are, by virtue of the Fall, depraved creatures. We do not believe, as did Martin Luther, that men and women are so inclined to evil that they do not have even the capacity to choose good on their own. We do not believe, as does much of the

Christian world, that because of the Fall little children are subject to an "original sin."

Sometimes as Latter-day Saints we get a little nervous about teaching the Fall, fretting perhaps that we might be misunderstood as accepting a belief in universal human depravity. We know it is true that all men and women are the literal spirit sons and daughters of a divine and exalted Father and that we have the capacity to become as he is.[5] It is wondrous indeed to contemplate the majesty of President Lorenzo Snow's doctrinal couplet:

> As Abra'm, Isaac, Jacob, too,
> First babes, then men—to gods they grew.
> As man now is, our God once was;
> As now God is, so man may be—
> Which doth unfold man's destiny.[6]

Having said all of that, having distanced ourselves from traditional Protestant and Catholic thought regarding the effects of Adam and Eve's transgression, I hasten to add that there was a fall and that the Fall does indeed take a measured toll on all mankind. It is real, and its effects cannot be ignored or its pull on the human heart mitigated by enlightened conversation. One's capacity to become as God is one thing; one's inclination to sin is quite another. It is only as men and women overcome many of the effects of the Fall through the atoning blood and ransoming power of Jesus Christ that they place themselves on the path to godhood.

In truth, to fail to teach the Fall is to lessen the effect of the Atonement. President Ezra Taft Benson observed: "Just as a man does not really desire food until he is hungry, so he does not desire the salvation of Christ until he knows why he needs Christ. No one adequately and properly knows why he needs Christ until he understands and accepts the doctrine of the Fall and its effect upon all mankind."[7] The Fall and the Atonement are a package deal; one brings the other into existence, and I am not aware of any discussion of the Atonement in the Book of Mormon that is not accompanied, either directly or by implication, with a discussion of the Fall. We do not appreciate and treasure the medicine until we appreciate the seriousness of the malady. One cannot look earnestly and longingly to the Redeemer if he or she does not sense the need for redemption. Jesus came to earth to do more than offer sage advice. He is not merely a benevolent consultant. He is our Savior. He came to save us.

The following represent but a few of the principles that may be derived from the Book of Mormon regarding the effects of the Fall and the nature of fallen humanity.

All mankind are lost and fallen. In what seems the very first reference in the Book of Mormon to the Fall, Nephi taught, "Six hundred years from the time that my father left Jerusalem, a prophet would the Lord God raise up among the Jews—even a Messiah, or, in other words, a Savior of the world. And he also spake concerning the prophets, how great a number had testified of these things, concerning this Messiah, of whom he had spoken, or this Redeemer of the world. Wherefore, all mankind were in a lost and in a fallen state, and ever would be save they should rely on this Redeemer" (1 Nephi 10:4–6; compare Alma 42:6). I am fascinated with the two words so descriptive of mortals—*lost* and *fallen.* Truly as Isaiah declared and as Abinadi quoted, "All we, like sheep, have gone astray; we have turned every one to his own way" (Mosiah 14:6; compare Isaiah 53:6). The Good Shepherd thus comes on a search-and-rescue mission after all of his lost sheep. He who never took a moral detour or a backward step thus reaches out and reaches down to lift us up. We are lost in the sense that we have wandered from a more exalted sphere; in the sense that we do not know our way home without a guide; in the sense that we are alienated from God and separated from things of righteousness. We are fallen in the sense that we have chosen, like our Exemplar, to condescend and enter a telestial tenement; in the sense that our eternal spirit, a spark of divinity struck from the fires of God's eternal blaze, has taken up its temporary abode in a tabernacle of clay; in the sense that we must be lifted up, quickened, and resuscitated spiritually if we are to return to the glorious place from whence we came.

Men and women are lost and fallen in that they are subject to spiritual death, the separation from God (see Alma 42:7, 9), the separation from things of righteousness (see Alma 12:16, 32; 40:26). Alma explained to Corianton that after partaking of the forbidden fruit, our first parents were "cut off from the tree of life" and thereby "became lost forever, yea, they became fallen man. And now, ye see by this that our first parents were cut off both temporally and spiritually from the presence of the Lord; and thus we see they became subjects to follow after their own will." Alma pointed out that inasmuch as "the fall had brought upon all mankind a spiritual death as well as a temporal, that is, they were cut off from the presence of the Lord, it was expedient that mankind should be reclaimed from this spiritual death. Therefore, as they had become carnal, sensual, and devilish, by nature, this probationary state became a state for them to prepare; it became a preparatory state" (Alma 42:6–10).

We inherit a fallen nature through conception. God spoke to Father Adam in the dawn of history: "Inasmuch as thy children are conceived in sin, even so when they begin to grow up, sin conceiveth in their hearts, and they taste the bitter, that they may know to prize the good" (Moses 6:55). In one sense, to be conceived in sin is to be conceived into a world of sin, to come forth into a telestial sphere, a state in which sin predominates. But there is more to it than that. Conception becomes the vehicle, the means whereby a fallen nature—mortality, what the scriptures call "the flesh"—is transmitted to the posterity of Adam and Eve. In short, to say that we are not responsible for the fall of Adam and Eve is not to say that we are unaffected by it. To say that we do not inherit an original sin through the Fall is not to say that we do not inherit a fallen nature and thus the capacity to sin. Fallenness and mortality are inherited. They come to us as a natural consequence of the second estate.

Lehi explained to Jacob that after the Fall "the days of the children of men were prolonged, according to the will of God, that they might repent while in the flesh; wherefore, their state became a state of probation, and their time was lengthened, according to the commandments which the Lord God gave unto the children of men. For he gave commandment that all men must repent; for he showed unto all men that they were lost, because of the transgression of their parents" (2 Nephi 2:21). Abinadi likewise explained to the priests of Noah that yielding to Lucifer's temptation in the Garden of Eden "was the cause of their [Adam and Eve's] fall; which [fall] was the cause of all mankind becoming carnal, sensual, devilish, knowing evil from good, subjecting themselves to the devil. Thus all mankind were lost; and behold, they would have been endlessly lost were it not that God redeemed his people from their lost and fallen state" (Mosiah 16:3–4). At this point in reading the passage, we might be tempted to breathe a sigh of relief and rejoice that the Fall is already taken care of because Jesus suffered and died. Unfortunately, Abinadi continues, and in so doing points out that the fallen nature is not just something we descend into through personal sin, but something out of which we must be extracted through divine regenerating powers. "But remember," he said, "that he that persists in his own carnal nature, and goes on in the ways of sin and rebellion against God, remaineth in his fallen state and the devil hath all power over him. Therefore he is as though there was no redemption made, being an enemy to God; and also is the devil an enemy to God" (Mosiah 16:5).

Elder Bruce R. McConkie wrote: "Adam fell. We know that this fall came because of transgression, and that Adam broke the law of God, became mortal, and was thus subject to sin and disease and all the ills of mortality. We know that the effects of his fall passed upon all his posterity; all inherited a fallen state, a state of mortality, a state in which temporal and spiritual death prevail. In this state all men sin. All are lost. All are fallen. All are cut off from the presence of God. All have become carnal, sensual, and devilish by nature. Such a way of life is inherent in this mortal existence."[8] Similarly, President Brigham Young noted that a critical and doubting disposition concerning the work of the Lord "arises from the power of evil that is so prevalent upon the face of the whole earth. It was given to you by your father and mother; it was mingled with your conception in the womb, and it has ripened in your flesh, in your blood, and in your bones, so that it has become riveted in your very nature."[9] On another occasion he explained: "There are no persons without evil passions to embitter their lives. Mankind are revengeful, passionate, hateful, and devilish in their dispositions. This we inherit through the fall, and the grace of God is designed to enable us to overcome it."[10]

One may be faithful and pure-hearted and yet still be buffeted by the pulls of a fallen world. Another way of stating this principle is that there is a difference between the natural man and the spiritual man who is taunted by the natural world in which he lives. Perhaps there is no better illustration in scripture than Nephi, son of Lehi. Here was a man who was obedient and submissive, a man who was led and empowered by the Spirit of Almighty God. "My soul delighteth in the things of the Lord," he wrote, "and my heart pondereth continually upon the things which I have seen and heard." Now note the following words, spoken by a man who was surely as pure and virtuous as anyone we know: "Nevertheless, notwithstanding the great goodness of the Lord, in showing me his great and marvelous works, my heart exclaimeth: O wretched man that I am! Yea, my heart sorroweth because of my flesh; my soul grieveth because of mine iniquities. I am encompassed about, because of the temptations and the sins which do so easily beset me. And when I desire to rejoice, my heart groaneth because of my sins" (2 Nephi 4:16–19).

The people of Benjamin were described by their great king as "a diligent people in keeping the commandments of the Lord" (Mosiah 1:11). We suppose they were members of The Church of Jesus Christ, followers of our Lord and Savior, people who had come out of the world by covenant. Benjamin delivered to his people one of the most significant addresses in all the Book of Mormon. He announced his own retirement and his son Mosiah as his successor, gave an accounting of his reign and ministry, encouraged the people to serve one another and thereby serve God, and counseled them (in the words of an angel) to put off the natural man and put on Christ through the Atonement. The people were electrified by the power of the message. Benjamin "cast his eyes round about on the multitude, and behold they had fallen to the earth, for the fear of the Lord had come upon them." And then this unusual insight: "And they had viewed themselves in their own carnal state, even less than the dust of the earth" (Mosiah 4:1–2). They cried unto the Lord for forgiveness and deliverance. Interesting, isn't it? A noble people, a diligent people who view themselves in their own carnal state.

In Moroni's abridgment of the Jaredite record, we discover that the brother of Jared encountered two major problems in his efforts to construct eight seaworthy vessels to transport his people to the promised land—air and light. We presume that the problem of ventilating the vessels was architecturally beyond the brother of Jared, for the Lord simply told him how to do it. But in regard to the light, Jehovah essentially asked: "Well, what would you have me to do?" implying that he expected Mahonri Moriancumr to do some homework. The Jaredite leader went to the top of Mount Shelem with sixteen transparent stones, eager to have the Lord touch them and thereby light their barges. He presented the stones to the Lord and prayed: "O Lord, thou hast said that we must be encompassed about by the floods. Now behold, O Lord, and do not be angry with thy servant because of his weakness before thee; for we know that thou art holy and dwellest in the heavens, and that we are unworthy before thee; because of the fall our natures have become evil continually" (Ether 3:2). He then called upon God for divine assistance.

We can grow in spiritual graces to the point wherein we have no more disposition to do evil but to do good continually (see Mosiah 5:2) and wherein we cannot look upon sin save it be with abhorrence (see Alma 13:12; see also 2 Nephi 9:49; Jacob 2:5). We can, like Nephi, delight in the things of the Lord (see 2 Nephi 4:16). But as long as we dwell in the flesh, we shall be subject to the pulls of a fallen world. "Will sin be perfectly destroyed?" President Brigham Young asked. "No, it will not, for it is not so designed in the economy of heaven. . . . Do not suppose that we shall ever in the flesh be free from temptations to sin. Some suppose that they can in the flesh be sanctified body and spirit and become so pure that they will never again feel the effects of the power of the adversary of truth. Were it possible for a person to attain to this degree of perfection in the flesh, he could not die neither remain in a world where sin predominates. . . . I think we shall more or less feel the effects of sin so long as we live, and finally have to pass the ordeals of death."[11]

Little children are innocent by virtue of the Atonement, not by nature. Joseph Smith's teachings concerning the innocence and salvation of little children—drawn from the Book of Mormon, his inspired translation of the Bible, and the revelations we now have in the Doctrine and Covenants—came as a refreshing breeze amidst the arid and sweltering winds of doctrinal corruption and confusion. But even in the restored Church there is some confusion on this matter. We ask, Are little children innocent? The answer is a resounding yes. But that question is not really a debated issue. We all know that little children are innocent. The more difficult point is: Why are little children innocent? Two possibilities suggest themselves. First, there are those who believe little children are innocent because they are that way by nature. They are pure and holy and decent and good and unselfish and solicitous and benevolent and submissive, just by virtue of being little children. The answer in the Book of Mormon and in modern revelation is that little children are innocent as one of the unconditional blessings of the Atonement because Jesus Christ decreed them so.

Benjamin, in citing the message of an angel, declared that "even if it were possible that little children could sin they could not be saved," meaning, presumably, if there had been no Atonement; "but I say unto you they are blessed; for behold, as in Adam, or by nature, they fall, even so the blood of Christ atoneth for their sins" (Mosiah 3:16). Mormon taught similarly that little children are innocent "even from the foundation of the world" and that "all little children are alive in Christ, and also all they that are without the law. For the power of redemption cometh on all them that have no law" (Moroni 8:12, 22). Modern revelation attests that "little children are redeemed from the foundation of the world through mine Only Begotten" (D&C 29:46) and that "little children are holy, being sanctified through the atonement of Jesus Christ" (D&C 74:7; compare JST Matthew 18:11; 19:13). We are thus encouraged to become as little children, not only in becoming submissive, meek, humble, patient, and full of love (see Mosiah 3:19) but also in becoming innocent through the atoning blood of Christ (see Moroni 8:10).

The natural man is an enemy to God and to all righteousness. "There is a natural birth, and there is a spiritual birth," Elder Bruce R. McConkie wrote. "The natural birth is to die as pertaining to premortal life, to leave the heavenly realms where all spirits dwell in the Divine Presence, and to begin a new life, a mortal life, a life here on earth. The natural birth creates a natural man, and the natural man is an enemy to God. In his fallen state he is carnal, sensual, and devilish by nature. Appetites and passions govern his life, and he is alive—acutely so—to all that is evil and wicked in the world."[12] The angel explained to Benjamin that "men drink damnation to their own souls except they humble themselves and become as little children, and believe that salvation was, and is, and is to come, in and through the atoning blood of Christ, the Lord Omnipotent. For the natural man is an enemy to God, and has been from the fall of Adam, and will be, forever and ever, unless he yields to the enticings of the Holy Spirit, and putteth off the natural man and becometh a saint through the atonement of Christ the Lord" (Mosiah 3:18–19).

The natural man is an enemy to God in that he (or she) is operating on an agenda other than God's; is doing everything in his power to bring to pass his own whims and wishes; in general, has placed his will above that of the Captain of his soul. President Brigham Young taught that "the natural man is at enmity with God. That fallen nature in every one is naturally opposed, inherently, through the fall, to God and to His Kingdom, and wants nothing to do with them."[13] Such persons are thereby operating at cross-purposes to the Father's plan for the salvation and redemption of his children and thus prove their own worst enemy as well. "All men that are in a state of nature," Alma observed, "or I would say, in a carnal state, are in the gall of bitterness and in the bonds of iniquity; they are without God in the world, and they have gone contrary to the nature of God; therefore, they are in a state contrary to the nature of happiness" (Alma 41:11).

The apostle Paul wrote to the Corinthian Saints that "the natural man receiveth not the things of the Spirit of God: for they are foolishness unto him: neither can he know them, because they are spiritually discerned" (1 Corinthians 2:14). In the process of rejoicing in God, Ammon spoke of the gratitude he felt that he and his brothers had not been cast off forever for going about to destroy the Church of God. "Behold, he did not exercise his justice upon us, but in his great mercy hath brought us over that everlasting gulf of death and misery, even to the salvation of our souls. And now behold, my brethren, what natural man is there that knoweth these things? I say unto you, there is none that knoweth these things, save it be the penitent" (Alma 26:20–21). President Young stated that "the natural man (or as we now use the language, the fallen or sinful man) receiveth not the things of the Spirit of God. . . . In no other way can the things of God be understood. Men who are destitute of the influence of the Holy Ghost, or the Spirit of God, cannot understand the things of God; they may read them, but to them they are shrouded in darkness."[14]

REDEMPTION FROM THE FALL

We have spoken of the malady, and now we turn to the cure. We have spoken of the bad news of the Fall and now turn to the good news, the glad tidings, of the Atonement.

Some years ago I sat with my counselors in a bishopric meeting. The session was drawing to a close because sacrament meeting would be starting in just ten minutes. A knock came at the door. A young woman from my ward asked if she could visit with me for a moment. I indicated to her that we could chat for a bit, but that sacrament meeting would be starting soon. She assured me that we would be together for only a minute or two. After we had been seated for a few seconds, she said: "Bishop, I need to confess a sin." I was startled with the suddenness of the statement, but, managing to maintain my composure, I offered, "Well, that could take some time, couldn't it? Shall we meet after the block of meetings today?" She quickly responded, "Oh no! This will just take a second."

She proceeded to describe a very serious moral transgression in which she had been involved. It was now about one minute before the meetings were to start, and so I tried again: "Why don't we get together after priesthood and Relief Society meetings?" She staggered me with, "Well, I don't know why we would need to, unless it would be helpful to you, or something." I indicated that such a meeting might prove beneficial to both of us. She agreed to return. Three hours later, and after we had exchanged a few pleasantries, I asked her, "How do you feel about what has happened?" She responded, "Just fine." I must have shown my perplexity because she added, "For a number of hours I felt bad about what had happened, but it's okay now because I've repented."

I couldn't ask her the question fast enough: "What do you mean when you say that you have repented?" She had explained to me earlier that the transgression had taken place on Friday night, and it was now Sunday afternoon. At that point, she reached into her purse and retrieved a yellow sheet of legal-size paper. Pointing one by one to various headings that began with an *R,* she said, "I've done this, and this, and this, and this, and finally I've confessed to you. I've repented."

"It seems to me that you've skipped an *R,* that your list is missing something," I said. I noted a startled look in her eyes and a slight impatience with me as she said, "No, that can't be. I have everything listed here!"

"The *R* you're missing," I responded, "is *Redeemer.* You have no place for Christ on your list. I mean, what does Jesus Christ have to do with your transgression? What does what happened in Gethsemane and on Calvary two thousand years ago have to do with what happened to you two nights ago?"

She answered: "Jesus died for me. He died for my sins."

To almost every question I asked thereafter she gave a perfectly correct answer. She had been well trained, and her answers reflected an awareness of the doctrines associated with repentance. But the answers were all totally cerebral, straight from memory and mind, not from the heart. She obviously saw no real tie between her own ungodly actions and the infinite actions of a God. We spent a few hours together that day and many days thereafter searching the scriptures, praying together, and counseling over the way back to the strait and narrow path. We talked often and intently about Jesus Christ. She came in time to know the correct answers by feeling—that is, from the heart.

Since that time, I have formulated my own brief list of *R*s, those that point my mind and rivet my affections to Jesus the Messiah. There is nothing sacred about this list (how many, what order, and so on), except that they direct my own heart to sacred things.

RESOLVING to come unto Christ. Some years ago it was not uncommon to see bumper stickers and placards that read "Jesus is the answer." As we suggested earlier, answers are always much more meaningful when we know the question. As was the case anciently in Alma's dealings with the Zoramites, so it is today. The great question is whether there is a Christ and what role he does or should have in our lives (see Alma 34:5).

Those who labor tirelessly to lighten burdens or alleviate human suffering but at the same time deny that Jesus Christ is God or deny the need for a Savior in this enlightened age cannot have the lasting effect on society that they could have through drawing upon the spiritual forces that center in the Lord Omnipotent. Those in our day who focus endlessly on the moral teachings of Jesus but who downplay the divine Sonship miss the mark dramatically. For some, Jesus stands as the preeminent example of kindness, the ultimate illustration of social and interpersonal graciousness and morality. A favorite text for them is the Sermon on the Mount; their highest aspiration is the call to live the Golden Rule. A Roman Catholic philosopher observed: "According to the theological liberal, this sermon [the Sermon on the Mount] is the essence of Christianity, and Christ is the best of human teachers and examples. . . . Christianity is essentially ethics. What's missing here?" he asks. "Simply, the essence of Christianity, which is *not* the

Sermon on the Mount. When Christianity was proclaimed throughout the world, the proclamation (*kerygma*) was not 'Love your enemies!' but 'Christ is risen!' This was not a new *ideal* but a new *event,* that God became man, died, and rose for our salvation. Christianity is first of all not ideal but real, an event, news, the gospel, the 'good news.' The essence of Christianity is not Christianity; the essence of Christianity is Christ."[15]

We come unto Christ not alone to be taught but to be transformed. He is not only our Example but also our Change Agent and our Benefactor. Jesus is not only a convenient resource; he is the vital and indispensible element in our quest for happiness here and eternal reward hereafter. There is no hope and no possibility of reconciliation with the Father except by and through the Savior.

Enos wrestled with his sins until he heard the voice of God declaring, "Enos, thy sins are forgiven thee, and thou shalt be blessed." "Lord, how is it done?" Enos asked. The Lord answered: "Because of thy faith in Christ, whom thou hast never before heard nor seen. . . . Wherefore, go to, thy faith hath made thee whole" (Enos 1:5–8). In his agony, confronted and tortured spiritually through the medium of memory, Alma the Younger reported:

> And it came to pass that as I was thus racked with torment, while I was harrowed up by the memory of my many sins, behold, I remembered also to have heard my father prophesy unto the people concerning the coming of one Jesus Christ, a Son of God, to atone for the sins of the world.
>
> Now, as my mind caught hold upon this thought, I cried within my heart: O Jesus, thou Son of God, have mercy on me, who am in the gall of bitterness, and am encircled about by the everlasting chains of death.
>
> And now, behold, when I thought this, I could

> remember my pains no more; yea, I was harrowed up by the memory of my sins no more.
>
> And oh, what joy, and what marvelous light I did behold; yea, my soul was filled with joy as exceeding as was my pain! [Alma 36:17–20]

Indeed, Jesus Christ is the Source of solace. Jesus Christ is the Prince of Peace.

A grand key to coming unto Christ is acknowledging the goodness and omnipotence of Christ. It consists of yielding our hearts unto him (see Helaman 3:35), submitting to his wisdom and omniscience. It is an unconditional surrender, an unqualified sacrifice of self on the altar of Christ. It is to hearken to the counsel of Amaleki: "And now . . . , I would that ye should come unto Christ, who is the Holy One of Israel, and partake of his salvation, and the power of his redemption. Yea, come unto him, and offer your whole souls as an offering unto him" (Omni 1:26). "Men and women who turn their lives over to God," President Ezra Taft Benson stated, "will discover that He can make a lot more out of their lives than they can. He will deepen their joys, expand their vision, quicken their minds, strengthen their muscles, lift their spirits, multiply their blessings, increase their opportunities, comfort their souls, raise up friends, and pour out peace."[16]

Being RECONCILED to God through Christ. The Fall brought changes to the earth and all forms of life on earth, changes both cosmic and personal. In the spiritual realm, men and women began life in a new sphere, a new state, a new kind of being. Whereas in Eden Adam and Eve had enjoyed the blessings of a terrestrial, immortal condition in which things were not subject to death, now on a fallen telestial earth all things began their steady decline toward dissolution. From modern revelation "we learn man's situation at his first creation, the knowledge with which he was endowed, and the high and exalted station in which he was placed—lord or governor of all things on earth, and at the same time enjoying communion . . . with his Maker, without a veil to separate between."[17] After the Fall, however, Adam and Eve "heard the voice of the Lord from the way toward the Garden of Eden, speaking unto them, and they saw him not; for they were shut out from his presence" (Moses 5:4; compare D&C 29:41).

The Atonement is that divine act of mercy and grace and condescension by which our Father and God opens the door to reunion. In and through Adam we partake of mortality and death. In and through Christ, our Mediator and Intercessor, we partake of immortality and the abundant life. By means of the Atonement we are reconciled to the Father. By means of the Atonement the finite is reconciled to the Infinite, the incomplete to the Complete, the unfinished to the Finished, the imperfect to the Perfect. Jacob pleaded: "Wherefore, . . . reconcile yourselves to the will of God, and not to the will of the devil and the flesh; and remember, after ye are reconciled unto God, that it is only in and through the grace of God that ye are saved" (2 Nephi 10:24). The Atonement, as an act of grace, demonstrates the love of the Father for his children. Jesus Christ, who lived a sinless and perfect life, claims of the Father "his rights of mercy which he hath upon the children of men" (Moroni 7:27). Jacob also reminded his people and us: "Wherefore, . . . seek not to counsel the Lord, but to take counsel from his hand. For behold, ye yourselves know that he counseleth in wisdom, and in justice, and in great mercy, over all his works. Wherefore, . . . be reconciled unto him through the atonement of Christ, his Only Begotten Son, and ye may obtain a resurrection, according to the power of the resurrection which is in

Christ, and be presented as the first-fruits of Christ unto God" (Jacob 4:10–11).

Being RENEWED in Christ. The Book of Mormon is a powerful invitation to come unto Christ and be changed. Indeed, one who chooses Christ chooses to be changed. The plan of salvation is not just a program bent on making bad men good and good men better; the Rotary Club can do that. Rather, it is a system of salvation that seeks to renovate society and transform the whole of humankind. The gospel of Jesus Christ is intended to make of earth a heaven and of man a god.

Those who are dead to the things of the Spirit must be quickened, made alive, or born again to enter the realm of divine experience. That is not optional; it is required. Elder McConkie has written: "The spiritual birth comes after the natural birth. It is to die as pertaining to worldliness and carnality and to become a new creature by the power of the Spirit. It is to begin a new life, a life in which we bridle our passions and control our appetites, a life of righteousness, a spiritual life. Whereas we were in a deep abyss of darkness, now we are alive in Christ and bask in the shining rays of his everlasting light. Such is the new birth, the second birth, the birth into the household of Christ."[18] The new birth is the means by which "the dark veil of unbelief" is removed from our minds and by which the "light of the glory of God" infuses joy into our souls (Alma 19:6). It is the process by which we "lay aside every sin, which easily doth beset [us], which doth bind [us] down to destruction" (Alma 7:15). It is the only way whereby we can receive the image of Christ in our countenances (see Alma 5:14).

The renewal of which we speak is a conversion from worldliness to saintliness, from being lured by the lurid to being enticed by holiness. It comes to us by virtue of the cleansing blood of Jesus and through the medium of the Holy Ghost, who is the Sanctifier. After hearing a powerful address, the people of Benjamin "cried with one voice, saying: Yea, we believe all the words which thou hast spoken unto us; and also, we know of their surety and truth, because of the Spirit of the Lord Omnipotent, which has wrought a mighty change in us, or in our hearts, that we have no more disposition to do evil, but to do good continually" (Mosiah 5:2; compare Alma 19:33). This conversion experience was real. It was born of the Spirit. It was of God. Surely as time passed and as the people grew into that meaningful spiritual union with Christ of which the prophets speak, there would be little in the world to recommend itself to them, for their desires were to please the Almighty and enjoy his approbation. We do not suppose, however, that the people of Benjamin never sinned again; that would be impossible in this fallen sphere. No, they sinned and made mistakes thereafter, but they had no desires to do so. And, thanks be to God, we shall be judged not only by our works but also by the desires of our hearts (see Alma 41:3; D&C 137:9).

The testimony of Alma the Younger is vital. Having lain immobile for three days and three nights and having come face to face with the heinous nature of his sins, he awoke to a new life. Alma "stood up and began to speak unto them, bidding them to be of good comfort: for, said he, I have repented of my sins, and have been redeemed of the Lord; behold I am born of the Spirit. And the Lord said unto me: Marvel not that all mankind, yea, men and women, all nations, kindreds, tongues, and people, must be born again; yea, born of God, changed from their carnal and fallen state, to a state of righteousness, being redeemed of God, becoming his sons and daughters; and thus they become new creatures; and unless they do this, they can in nowise inherit the kingdom of God" (Mosiah 27:23–26).

President Ezra Taft Benson noted that "we must be careful, as we seek to become more and more godlike, that we do not become discouraged and lose hope. Becoming Christlike is a lifetime pursuit and very often involves growth and change that is slow, almost imperceptible." Then, after talking about the sudden spiritual transformations of such notables as Alma the Younger, Paul, Enos, and King Lamoni, he admonished: "We must be cautious as we discuss these remarkable examples. *Though they are real and powerful, they are the exception more than the rule.* For every Paul, for every Enos, and for every King Lamoni, there are hundreds and thousands of people who find the process of repentance much more subtle, much more imperceptible. Day by day they move closer to the Lord, little realizing they are building a godlike life. They live quiet lives of goodness, service, and commitment. They are like the Lamanites, who, the Lord said, 'were baptized with fire and with the Holy Ghost, and they knew it not' (3 Nephi 9:20)."[19]

Being REINSTATED in the family of God. The Fall distances us from righteousness and alienates us from the family of God. We come into this fallen world nameless and familyless. The Atonement therefore provides the means for forgiveness of sins and also of reinstatement in the royal family. Benjamin acknowledged this marvelous truth when he commended his people for their willingness to renew their baptismal covenant and come again unto Christ.

> And now, because of the covenant which ye have made ye shall be called the children of Christ, his sons, and his daughters; for behold, this day he hath spiritually begotten you; for ye say that your hearts are changed through faith on his name; therefore, ye are born of him and have become his sons and his daughters.

> And under this head ye are made free, and there is no other head whereby ye can be made free. There is no other name given whereby salvation cometh; therefore, I would that ye should take upon you the name of Christ, all you that have entered into the covenant with God that ye should be obedient unto the end of your lives. [Mosiah 5:7–8; compare 27:25]

Just as the newborn in our mortal world automatically enters into a family relationship through birth, so the new birth, the birth of the Spirit, becomes an avenue of life into the family of the Lord Jesus Christ. Christ is thus the Father of our awakening into newness of life, the Father of our resurrection, the Father of our salvation. We take his name upon us and seek to be worthy of that holy name. As members of his family we are expected to know who we are and act accordingly—to keep his commandments with fidelity and devotion and to take seriously our divine birthright as Christians. Thus we, as the seed of Christ, hearken unto the word of the prophets, look to Jesus our Lord for redemption, and publish peace after the manner of our Prince of Peace (see Mosiah 15:11–18). He is the Shepherd, and we are the sheep of his fold. "Behold, I say unto you, that the good shepherd doth call you; yea, and in his own name he doth call you, which is the name of Christ; and if ye will not hearken unto the voice of the good shepherd, to the name by which ye are called, behold, ye are not the sheep of the good shepherd" (Alma 5:38).

RELYING on the merits and mercy of Christ. The Book of Mormon teaches that we are saved by merit, but not our own merit. "Since man had fallen," Aaron explained to the father of Lamoni, "he could not merit anything of himself; but the sufferings and death of Christ atone for their sins, through faith and repentance, and so forth" (Alma 22:14). This passage requires a bit of explanation.

Of course we are expected to receive the ordinances of salvation, work faithfully in the kingdom, perform acts of Christian service, and endure faithfully to the end. Of course we are expected to do the works of righteousness. These things are necessary—they evidence our covenant with Christ to follow him and keep his commandments. They are *necessary,* but they are not *sufficient.*

We are expected to do the best we can, to give our whole service to our Master and our whole heart and soul to the cause of righteousness in the earth. But in the end it will not be enough. There are not enough cakes and pies and home teaching visits to make and meetings to attend and prayers to offer and temple ordinances to perform. We cannot, simply cannot, save ourselves. Our merits, no matter how godlike and consistent, will not qualify us for the highest heaven. Truly, as Lehi explained, "there is no flesh that can dwell in the presence of God, save it be through the merits, and mercy, and grace of the Holy Messiah" (2 Nephi 2:8). "Wherefore, I know that thou art redeemed," Lehi explained to his son Jacob. Why was he redeemed? Because of his faithfulness, his submissiveness, his willingness, like Nephi, to follow the counsel of his father? No. Jacob was redeemed "because of the righteousness of thy Redeemer" (2 Nephi 2:3).

The prophet Abinadi scathingly denounced Noah and his priests, particularly for the manner in which they feigned allegiance to the law of Moses but failed to live in harmony with its moral precepts. Further, he corrected their false impression that salvation could come by the law alone. "I say unto you," he declared, "that it is expedient that ye should keep the law of Moses as yet; but I say unto you, . . . that salvation doth not come by the law alone; and were it not for the atonement, which God himself shall make for the sins and iniquities of his people, that they must unavoidably perish, notwithstanding the law of Moses" (Mosiah 13:27–28).

Elder Bruce R. McConkie suggested a latter-day application of Abinadi's words:

> Suppose we have the scriptures, the gospel, the priesthood, the Church, the ordinances, the organization, even the keys of the kingdom—everything that now is down to the last jot and tittle—and yet there is no atonement of Christ. What then? Can we be saved? Will all our good works save us? Will we be rewarded for all our righteousness?
>
> Most assuredly we will not. We are not saved by works alone, no matter how good; we are saved because God sent his Son to shed his blood in Gethsemane and on Calvary that all through him might ransomed be. We are saved by the blood of Christ.
>
> To paraphrase Abinadi: Salvation doth not come by the church alone: and were it not for the atonement, given by the grace of God as a free gift, all men must unavoidably perish, and this notwithstanding the Church and all that appertains to it.[20]

The issue is not whether we are saved by works or by grace. Both are necessary. The real questions to be asked are, In whom do I trust? On whom do I rely? If I trust in my own works or rely on the labors of my own hands—no matter how noble they may be—I am propping my ladder against the wrong wall. If my confidence is in my capacity to "handle it myself," then my perspective is skewed and my hope is misplaced. Our reliance must be *wholly* upon the "merits of him who is mighty to save" (2 Nephi 31:19), *alone* upon "the merits of Christ, who [is] the author and the finisher of our faith" (Moroni 6:4). We are saved by the grace of Christ "after all we can do" (2 Nephi 25:23), meaning above and beyond all we can do. In the words of C. S. Lewis, those who come unto Christ learn that they cannot do it themselves but must leave it to God. Lewis says:

> The sense in which a Christian leaves it to God is that he puts all his trust in Christ: trusts that Christ will somehow share with him the perfect human obedience which He carried out from His birth to His crucifixion: that Christ will make the man more like Himself and, in a sense, make good his deficiencies. . . . And, in yet another sense, handing everything over to Christ does not, of course, mean that you stop trying. To trust Him means, of course, trying to do all that He says. There would be no sense in saying you trusted a person if you would not take his advice. Thus if you have really handed yourself over to Him, it must follow that *you are trying to obey Him. But trying in a new way, a less worried way.*[21]

RETAINING a remission of sins. It is a marvelous thing to know that through the cleansing powers of the blood of Christ we may obtain a remission of sins and thus stand spotless before God. The promise of forgiveness is indeed a miracle, a wondrous act on the part of a merciful and omniloving God. We know we are forgiven as the Spirit of the Lord returns and as joy and peace of conscience fill our souls once more (see Mosiah 4:1–3). And yet we stand each day, as it were, precariously, on the edge of a cliff—we are subject to subsequent sin. How can we, without trifling with repentance, remain pure?

The Book of Mormon prophets provide the answer. They speak of remaining in a justified condition, of maintaining or retaining our spotless standing before God even though we make mistakes. Like the people of Benjamin, we may err after our covenant with the Master, but we have no desire to do so. That is, our heart, our affections, our desires have all been surrendered unto Christ, and we have no desire to stray from our binding covenant with him. As we endure to the end through living constantly in a state of repentance with an ever-present desire to be transformed in Christ, the Savior holds us guiltless (see 3 Nephi 27:16; compare D&C 4:2).

Benjamin explained two means by which the Saints are enabled to retain a remission of sins from day to day. First of all, he said:

> As ye have come to the knowledge of the glory of God, or if ye have known of his goodness and have tasted of his love, and have received a remission of your sins, which causeth such exceedingly great joy in your souls, even so I would that ye should remember, and always retain in remembrance, the greatness of God, and your own nothingness, and his goodness and long-suffering towards you, unworthy creatures, and humble yourselves even in the depths of humility, calling on the name of the Lord daily, and standing steadfastly in the faith of that which is to come, which was spoken by the mouth of the angel.
>
> And behold, I say unto you that *if ye do this ye shall always rejoice, and be filled with the love of God, and always retain a remission of your sins;* and ye shall grow in the knowledge of the glory of him that created you, or in the knowledge of that which is just and true. [Mosiah 4:11–12; emphasis added; compare Moroni 7:42–44]

Acknowledgment of God's greatness and goodness, recognition of our absolute ineptitude without divine assistance, surrender to the sobering verity that our spiritual condition is bankrupt without the Atonement—these are the conditions for redemption in Christ, the means whereby we retain a remission of sins from day to day. Surely to the degree that we bow in humble reverence before the Lord Omnipotent and trust in his incomparable might, to that degree we open ourselves to the sweet enabling power we know as the grace of God.

That power serves not only as a final spiritual boost into exaltation hereafter but also as a significant means for the renovation of our character and personality in this life, the power behind the process wherein we become "partakers of the divine nature" (2 Peter 1:4) and evidence the "fruit of the Spirit" (Galatians 5:22–25).

The second means of retaining a remission of sins is set forth by King Benjamin after his lengthy plea with the people of God to look to the care of the needy. "And now, for the sake of these things which I have spoken unto you—that is, for the sake of retaining a remission of your sins from day to day, that ye may walk guiltless before God—I would that ye should impart of your substance to the poor, every man according to that which he hath, such as feeding the hungry, clothing the naked, visiting the sick and administering to their relief, both spiritually and temporally, according to their wants" (Mosiah 4:26).

Perhaps these two matters are really one; that is, the more I look to the Lord, humble myself before him, freely acknowledge his goodness and grace, and strive to be like him, the more I am inclined to look to the welfare of my brothers and sisters about me. Being filled with the love of God results in meaningful and lasting service to the children of God.

Mormon spoke of a time in the Nephite church's history when the pride and wickedness of the members proved to be "a great stumbling-block to those who did not belong to the church; and thus the church began to fail in its progress." On the other hand, "others were abasing themselves, succoring those who stood in need of their succor, such as imparting their substance to the poor and the needy, feeding the hungry, and suffering all manner of afflictions for Christ's sake, who should come according to the spirit of prophecy; looking forward to that day, thus retaining a remission of their sins;

being filled with great joy because of the resurrection of the dead, according to the will and power and deliverance of Jesus Christ from the bands of death" (Alma 4:10, 13–14).

CONCLUSION

We might go on and on in listing different *R*s of regeneration in Christ. But I desire to close with the *R* of *REJOICING in Christ.* Jacob surely sang the song of redeeming love (see Alma 5:26) when he gloried in the wisdom, goodness, greatness, justice, mercy, and holiness of our God (see 2 Nephi 9:8, 10, 17, 19, 20). Ammon boasted not in his own strength but in the infinite power of his Lord: "Yea, I know that I am nothing; as to my strength I am weak; therefore I will not boast of myself, but I will boast of my God, for in his strength I can do all things" (Alma 26:12).

I rejoice in the great plan of happiness and in the satisfaction that comes from the knowledge that God does indeed have a plan and that there is purpose in all we experience in this life. I rejoice that Adam fell that we might be (see 2 Nephi 2:25) and that because of that fall, all of us enter into mortality to undertake the second phase of our eternal journey. I rejoice in the Fall, for it brought forth the Atonement, the means whereby our hearts might be cleansed and our souls transformed and prepared to dwell with Christ and our Eternal Father.

I know of the malady we call the fallen condition and of the heartache that comes to us as we yield to the flesh. I also know of the consummate peace that comes as we strive to put off the natural man through the Atonement and yield to the enticings of the Holy Spirit. Thus "we talk of Christ, we rejoice in Christ, we preach of Christ, we prophesy of Christ, . . . that our children may know to what source they may look for a remission of their sins" (2 Nephi 25:26). Like Nephi, "I glory in plainness; I glory in truth; I glory in my Jesus, for he hath redeemed my soul from hell" (2 Nephi 33:6). Of that supernal truth I testify. For that good news, those glad tidings, I am immeasurably grateful.

NOTES

1. William R. Bradford, "Message Sublime," in *Brigham Young University 1982–83 Fireside and Devotional Speeches* (Provo, Utah: Brigham Young University, 1983), 156.

2. William R. Bradford, in Conference Report, Oct. 1983, 100–101.

3. Joseph Smith, *Teachings of the Prophet Joseph Smith,* sel. Joseph Fielding Smith (Salt Lake City: Deseret Book, 1976), 12.

4. Forace Green, comp., *Cowley and Whitney on Doctrine* (Salt Lake City: Bookcraft, 1963), 287.

5. See Smith, *Teachings of the Prophet Joseph Smith,* 346–48; Joseph Smith, *Lectures on Faith* (Salt Lake City: Deseret Book, 1985), 5:3.

6. Lorenzo Snow, 11 June 1892, in *Improvement Era,* June 1919, 660. See also Lorenzo Snow, *The Teachings of Lorenzo Snow,* comp. Clyde J. Williams (Salt Lake City: Bookcraft, 1984).

7. Ezra Taft Benson, *A Witness and a Warning* (Salt Lake City: Deseret Book, 1988), 33.

8. Bruce R. McConkie, *The Promised Messiah* (Salt Lake City: Deseret Book, 1978), 244.

9. Brigham Young, in *Journal of Discourses,* 26 vols. (London: Latter-day Saints' Book Depot, 1854–86), 2:134.

10. Brigham Young, in *Journal of Discourses,* 8:160.

11. Brigham Young, in *Journal of Discourses,* 10:173.

12. Bruce R. McConkie, *A New Witness for the Articles of Faith* (Salt Lake City: Deseret Book, 1985), 282.

13. Brigham Young, in *Journal of Discourses,* 12:323.

14. Brigham Young, in *Journal of Discourses,* 9:330.

15. Peter Kreeft, *Back to Virtue* (San Francisco: Ignatius Press, 1992), 83.

16. Ezra Taft Benson, *Teachings of Ezra Taft Benson* (Salt Lake City: Bookcraft, 1988), 361.

17. Smith, *Lectures on Faith,* 2:12.

18. McConkie, *New Witness,* 282.

19. Ezra Taft Benson, "A Mighty Change of Heart," *Ensign,* Oct. 1989, 2–5; emphasis added.

20. Bruce R. McConkie, "What Think Ye of Salvation by Grace?" in *Brigham Young University 1983–84 Fireside and Devotional Speeches* (Provo, Utah: Brigham Young University, 1984), 48.

21. C. S. Lewis, *Mere Christianity* (New York: Macmillan, 1952), 128–29; emphasis added.

CHAPTER FIVE

THE POWER OF EVIDENCE IN THE NURTURING OF FAITH

JOHN W. WELCH

Sidney Branton Sperry, whose one-hundredth birthday we commemorate this season, sought, found, and enjoyed publishing evidences in support of the scriptures, especially the Book of Mormon. What spiritual value do such evidences have? How do bits of knowledge contribute to an increase of faith? How do reason and revelation work together? What is evidence and how is it related to faith? Without diminishing the essential power of the Holy Ghost in bearing testimony, and knowing that we cannot prove anything in absolute terms, I still speak favorably about the power of evidence. It is an important ingredient in Heavenly Father's plan of happiness.

BOTH REASON AND REVELATION

Basic to the discussion of evidence and faith is the relationship between reason and revelation. One of my favorite scriptures is Doctrine and Covenants 88:118, a text that is posted conspicuously on a plaque in the old

John W. Welch is professor of law and founder of the Foundation for Ancient Research and Mormon Studies (FARMS) at Brigham Young University.

stairwell between the third and fourth floors of the Harold B. Lee Library: "As all have not faith, seek ye diligently and teach one another words of wisdom; yea, seek ye out of the best books words of wisdom; seek learning, even by study and also by faith." We would do well to post this verse in our own library. This passage gives significant place to the role of scholarship in the restored Church. It commands us to "seek" (which would include doing research) and to seek "diligently" (we must do it thoroughly and carefully); it obligates us to teach one another (to share our findings generously) and to draw out of "the best books" (which cautions us that some books will be better than others); and it tells us to do all this "even by study and also by faith" (in other words, both are required). Nothing is more fundamental for a Latter-day Saint scholar than to maintain a proper balance between the intellectual and spiritual pursuits of life.

Many Church leaders and authors have written about study and faith, and everyone agrees that we should have both.[1] President Gordon B. Hinckley has said: "There is incumbent upon each of us . . . the responsibility to observe the commandment to study and to learn. . . . None of us can assume that we have learned enough."[2] Elder Neal A. Maxwell has affirmed: "If there is sometimes too little respect for the life of the mind, it is a localized condition and is not institutional in character."[3] "The Lord sees no conflict between faith and learning in a broad curriculum. . . . The scriptures see faith and learning as mutually facilitating, not separate processes."[4] Elder Boyd K. Packer has said: "Each of us must accommodate the mixture of reason and revelation in our lives. The gospel not only permits but *requires* it."[5]

The difficult problem is not whether to have both study and faith but how to get these two together and in what order of priority or in what type of combination.

In attempting to describe or prescribe the proper coordination of study with faith, LDS thinkers have turned or may turn to various analogies, as we often must when we are confronted with our deepest intellectual or religious concepts. Each of these metaphors is potentially quite powerful. Some work better than others, but each may offer insight into the roles of scholarly evidence in nurturing or strengthening faith.

Some analogies emphasize that both study and faith are necessary. In the bicycle-built-for-two metaphor, the relationship between reason and revelation is likened to two riders on a tandem bicycle. When both riders pedal together, the bicycle (the search for truth) moves ahead more rapidly. Each rider must work, or the other must bear a heavy and perhaps exhausting burden; but only one (that is faith) can steer and determine where the bicycle will go, although the other (reason) can do some backseat driving.

In another metaphor, these two necessary elements are brought together as in a marriage, with "all the tension, adjustments, frustration, joys, and ecstasy one finds in a marriage between man and woman."[6]

Similarly, the apostle Paul used the human body as a strong metaphor to show the need for many parts in an organic whole. It would be unseemly for "the head [to say] to the feet, I have no need of you"; they are "many members, yet but one body" (1 Corinthians 12:20–21). As B. H. Roberts has cautioned, let us not have "the heart breathing defiance to the intellect."[7] And one might equally add, let us also not have the intellect pounding submission to the heart.

SOME EXAMPLES

A few studies may illustrate the function of evidence in building faith. The first is a new prospect that has intrigued me only recently. I am not yet entirely sure what to make of it. It comes from the use of doubled, sealed legal documents in ancient Israelite law. Because ancient peoples did not have copy machines or county recorders' offices, they often prepared important legal documents in duplicate, one part of the scroll being either a verbatim duplicate or an abridgment of the other. The open portion was available for routine inspection and daily use; the sealed portion was saved for use in court to resolve disputes or in case the open part got damaged or altered. The earliest known example of this practice using papyrus or parchment comes from Jerusalem and dates to around the time of Lehi, when Jeremiah wrote out a double deed, one part of which "was sealed according to the law and custom," and the other part "which was open" (Jeremiah 32:11). Subsequent examples of such legal documents have been found as this practice spread to Hellenistic Egypt and all around the eastern Mediterranean and the Roman empire.[8] Jewish law required at least three witnesses in order for such a doubled, sealed document to be valid. There could be additional witnesses, often totaling six or more.

The potential parallel with the Book of Mormon is quite striking. Nephi envisioned from the beginning that the Nephite record would eventually be a two-part book, consistent with the pattern of this Israelite law and custom. As early as about 550 B.C., Nephi described the time when the Book of Mormon would come forth, having two parts: the open part, the "words which are not sealed," he said, were to be delivered to Joseph Smith (2 Nephi 27:15); but Joseph would be told to "touch not the things which are sealed" (2 Nephi 27:21). The open part was, in a sense, less complete than the sealed part (see Ether 4:5). Three witnesses were specifically contemplated and others were promised and provided to "testify to the truth of the book and the things therein"

(2 Nephi 27:12; see also Ether 5:4). At the judgment bar, God will show that the things found in the open part are true (see Moroni 10:29). Although this doubled, sealed document practice was not understood well even in Jeremiah 32 until this century, and although nothing like it was used in American legal practice, it is right at home in Nephi's Jerusalem and seems to offer a possible explanation for the idea behind the construction and assembly of the Book of Mormon plates.

One might wonder if this procedure was ever used anciently in documents written on metal plates. Although the procedures had to be modified slightly to accommodate metal, a pair of bronze plates from the Roman Emperor Vespasian features a doubled text, witnessed by seven witnesses, and the two plates were sealed together with one text open and the other protected.[9] Does the mere possibility of this rather intriguing scenario begin to "arouse the faculties of your souls"? (Jacob 3:11; see also Alma 32:27). Might it contribute to your sphere of faith?

Many other studies of numerous types could be mentioned with similar effect. To name only a few that may be familiar, fascinating evidence for the Book of Mormon has been found in the last few years in such things as the semantic ranges of words like *thief* and *robber:* the meaning of the word *robber* in the Book of Mormon squares on all counts with its meaning in the ancient world.[10] The associated words *statute* and *ordinance* never happen to appear together in pleonastic lists in the Book of Mormon; neither do their Hebrew counterparts appear together in such lists in the Hebrew Bible.[11] Etymologies of several proper nouns in the Book of Mormon are intriguing (consider the word *Jershon* in Alma 27:22, which was given as a "land . . . for an inheritance," the name itself meaning in Hebrew, "a place of inheritance"). Word distributions show multiple authorship; for example, thirty phrases or expressions appear in Zenos's allegory in Jacob 5 that never again turn up in all four standard works.[12] The accuracies of internal quotations are uncanny: Alma 36:22 quotes Lehi's words in 1 Nephi 1:8, and Samuel the Lamanite in Helaman 14:12 quotes Benjamin's words in Mosiah 3:8 with inexplicable precision, given the circumstances—to name only a few examples that could be mentioned. Sidney Sperry was especially eager to point out that the Book of Mormon features many literary genres, showing that it was written by many people, as was the Bible.[13] He also enjoyed saying that "the Book of Mormon *is* a translation,"[14] that "it is not English freely composed but is rather the type of English that would be produced by a translator who frequently follows the original too closely,"[15] and that "the text proper shows the strong influence of Hebrew."[16]

Do points like these build faith? Although we should not expect to find a sign somewhere that says "Nephi slept here" or a drop of blood on the Mount of Olives that establishes the truth of Christ's ordeal in Gethsemane,[17] the world has been told to expect circumstantial evidences of the truth. An 1842 editorial announcing some archaeological discoveries in Central America that was published in the *Times and Seasons* when Joseph Smith was editor boldly asserts: "We can not but think the Lord has a hand in bringing to pass his strange act, and proving the Book of Mormon true in the eyes of all the people. . . . It will be as it ever has been, the world will prove Joseph Smith a true prophet by circumstantial evidence, in experiments, as they did Moses and Elijah."[18]

SPECIFIC WAYS EVIDENCE NURTURES FAITH

Without overstating the value of these factors, evidence plays several specific roles in the cultivation of faith. Comments by General Authorities and personal experiences by many people are instructive and have affirmed various functions.

Elder John A. Widtsoe taught that evidence can remove honest doubt and give assurances that build faith. "After proper inquiries, using all the powers at our command," he said, "the weight of evidence is on one side or the other. Doubt is removed."[19] "Doubt of the right kind—that is, honest questioning—leads to faith" and "opens the door to truth,"[20] for where there is doubt, faith cannot thrive. Elder Joseph Fielding Smith likewise affirmed that evidence, as convincing as in any court in the land, proves "beyond the possibility of doubt that Joseph Smith and Oliver Cowdery spoke the truth."[21]

Over and over, I have found that solid research confirms the revelations of God. As Elder Maxwell has stated, "That a truth is given by God and then is confirmed through scholarship makes it no less true."[22] President Hinckley has said that in a world prone to demand evidence, it is good that archaeology, anthropology, or historical research can "be helpful to some" and "confirmatory."[23]

Evidence also makes the truth plain and plausible. In 1976, Elder Maxwell predicted: "There will be a convergence of discoveries (never enough, mind you, to remove the need for faith) to make plain and plausible what the modern prophets have been saying all along."[24] I believe that this prophecy has been amply fulfilled in the last twenty years. Literally hundreds of newly discovered insights converge on the same supporting conclusion. Certain things that might at first have appeared outrageous, on closer inspection have turned out to be right on target. The ancient Jaredite transoceanic migration that lasted 344 days (see Ether 6:11) ceases to seem so fantastic when that turns out to be exactly the length of time it takes the Pacific current to go from Asia to

Mexico.[25] The oddity of Nephi's making new arrows when only his bow had broken suddenly becomes plausible when one realizes that arrows and bows must match each other in weight, length, and stiffness.[26] The bizarre ritual of chopping down the tree as part of Zemnarihah's execution (see 3 Nephi 4:28) fits right into place in light of Jewish law that required the tree to be chopped down on which a person was hanged,[27] again making "plain and plausible" what the Book of Mormon has said all along.

In an important sense, evidence makes belief possible. I am very impressed by the words of Austin Farrar in speaking about C.S. Lewis and quoted by Elder Maxwell on several occasions: "Though argument does not create conviction, lack of it destroys belief. What seems to be proved may not be embraced; but what no one shows that ability to defend is quickly abandoned. Rational argument does not create belief, but it maintains a climate in which belief may flourish."[28]

Thus, evidence in a sense brings people toward belief. Some people have the gift to believe quite readily (see D&C 46:13–14), but most people need evidence, clues, and inducements to believe because they are by nature stubborn. Alma told the poor in Antionum that it was blessed to believe in the word of God "without stubbornness of heart, yea, without being brought to know the word, or even compelled to know" (Alma 32:16); but being "brought to know" is better than never coming to know at all. I have been "brought to know" many things by means of evidence, even though that evidence has fallen short of compelling me to know.

Evidence is also useful in articulating knowledge and defending against error and misrepresentation. Scholars can serve important roles "as articulators" of evidence, and when combined with "submissiveness and consecration," solid academic research can be useful "to protect and to build up the Kingdom."[29] If people misunderstand the thoroughly Christian character of the Book of Mormon, I would hope that statistical evidence about the pervasive references to Christ in the book would be quite arresting and informative.[30] I would hope that evidence about the distinctively personal testimonies of Christ uniquely borne by ten Book of Mormon prophets would be deeply impressive and convincing.[31]

Evidence helps to keep pace in the give-and-take of competing alternatives: Do you expect "incontrovertible proof to come in this way? No, but neither will the Church be outdone by hostile or pseudo-scholars."[32] The historical facts in support of Joseph's testimony, to quote Elder Jeffrey R. Holland, leave one "speechless—absolutely, totally, and bewilderingly incredulous," at the bald suggestion that Joseph Smith simply wrote the Book of Mormon.[33]

Perhaps most of all, in my opinion, evidence promotes understanding and enhances meaning. In all our study, we should seek understanding.[34] Just as traveling to the Holy Land has richly enhanced my understanding of the world of the Bible, as it has for many people, evidence provides essential building blocks in understanding the full character of the Book of Mormon. Many factors, like the doubled, sealed documents, help me understand this record better as a powerful and ancient testament, for to be understood, our facts must be placed "in their proper context."[35] Evidence helps to put many parts of the Book of Mormon in context. Thus, we understand Nephi's slaying of Laban in its proper ancient and divine contexts when we consider the meaning and implications of Exodus 21:13–14, which in Nephi's day defined excusable slayings differently from the way we do today.[36]

A clear delineation of evidence also strengthens the

impression left by any text on the mind and soul. Evidence has a way of drawing my attention to subtle details that otherwise escape notice on casual reading. With evidence about ancient Israelite festivals in mind, I read with heightened attention and gratitude the text in Mosiah 3:11 about Christ's blood atoning for those who have "ignorantly sinned," because it was of primary concern on ancient holy days to purify the people from all their iniquities (see Leviticus 16:21–22), with special reference being made to sins committed in ignorance (see Numbers 15:22–29).[37]

Marshalling evidence builds respect for the truth. I have been amazed and pleased to watch the Book of Mormon win respect for itself and for the gospel of Jesus Christ. I had long appreciated and valued the Book of Mormon, but it was not until I began to see it speaking for itself before sophisticated audiences, especially in connection with such things as chiasmus and law in the Book of Mormon, that I began to sense the high level of respect which the book really can command. On many grounds, the Book of Mormon is intellectually respectable.[38] The more I learn about the Book of Mormon, the more amazed I become at its precision, consistency, validity, vitality, insightfulness, and purposefulness. I believe that the flow of additional evidence nourishes and enlarges faith.[39]

Finally, the presentation of evidence impels people to ask the ultimate question raised by that evidence. Once a person realizes that no one can explain how all this got into the Book of Mormon, the honest person is at last at the point where he or she must turn to God to find out if these things are indeed true. Elder Bruce R. McConkie advised readers to ask themselves over and over, a thousand times, "Could any man have written this book?"[40] By asking this question again and again, one invites all kinds of ideas that may bear one way or the other on the answer to that question. As ideas surface, evidence can help the reader explore those possibilities and inevitably return with increased intensity to the question, "Could any man have written this book?" If one will ponder the great miracle of the Book of Mormon, Elder McConkie promises, "the genuine truth seeker will come to know," again and again, "by the power of the Spirit, that the book is true."[41]

Moroni 10:3–4 promises this testimony but on several prerequisites: one must "read these things" (one must study it); one must "remember how merciful the Lord hath been"; and one must "ponder" this record. Then "if ye shall ask with a sincere heart, with real intent, having faith in Christ," the answer will be revealed. Many people have told me how evidences have helped to impel them through this process of reading, studying, pondering, and asking.

The Holy Ghost bears record of the Father and of the Son (see 3 Nephi 11:32, 36). Scripturally, this truth is beyond question. Elder B. H. Roberts wrote in 1909: "The power of the Holy Ghost . . . must ever be the chief source of evidence for the truth of the Book of Mormon. All other evidence is secondary. . . . No arrangement of evidence, however skillfully ordered; no argument, however adroitly made, can ever take its place."[42] It would certainly be an abuse to supplant testimony and faith with evidence, or with anything else, but scrutinizing evidence can help. Elder Roberts continued: "Evidence and argument . . . in support of truth, like secondary causes in natural phenomena, may be of first rate importance, and mighty factors in the achievement of God's purposes."[43] Indeed, the careful presentation of evidence clarifies the truth and enhances the power of testimony. Elder Roberts concluded: "To be known, the truth must be stated and the clearer and more complete the statement is, the better opportunity will the Holy

Spirit have for testifying to the souls of men that the work is true."[44]

STUDY AND FAITH WORKING TOGETHER

In all of these faith-promoting functions, it is not enough just to have one's mind and one's spirit both alive and functioning; the two must work together, each contributing in its own proper way. To turn to another metaphor, the correlation of faith and reason works like our two eyes (representing mind and spirit); working together they give depth to our sight, and with the aid of a pair of binoculars (representing scholarship and revelation), we see close up and in bold relief many marvelous things. For this process to work, however, both eyes must be healthy and both lenses in the binoculars must be clean and in focus.

I also like to think of faith and reason as two arms working together to play a violin. One hand fingers the strings and the other draws the bow. When these two distinct functions are brought together with skill and purpose, they produce expressions that ontologically transcend the physics of either part individually. According to this view, for an LDS scholar to proceed on either spirit or intellect alone is like trying to play a violin with only one arm.

GAINING FAITH IN GENERAL

Nurturing faith in the Book of Mormon is just a specialized case of nurturing faith in general. Faith is increased by purposeful study, diligent prayer, attending church, rendering service, experimenting with the word, and feeling the Spirit. Evidence can play a role in this process in several ways.

First, Paul declared: "So then faith cometh by hearing, and hearing by the word of God" (Romans 10:17). The presentation of evidence can help people to hear the word, to pay attention, to listen more closely, to hear what is really being said. King Benjamin admonished his people to "open your ears that ye may hear, and your hearts that ye may understand, and your minds that the mysteries of God may be unfolded to your view" (Mosiah 2:9). I have seen evidence, when it is presented modestly and accurately, help people listen to the Book of Mormon who otherwise would not give it the time of day. I have seen it soften hearts and prepare the way for testimony to be borne and received.

Second, faith comes by prayerful study. In the words of President Hinckley: "It will take study of the word of God. It will take prayer and anxious seeking of the source of all truth."[45] The study of scriptural evidence can be a vital aid in this process, for faith is only faith if it is in things "which are true" (Alma 32:21). The intelligent use of evidence helps people sort out propositions that are clear, true, or plausible from those that are muddled, false, or bogus.

Third, faith also comes from sacrifice. For Elder McConkie, "faith and sacrifice go hand in hand. Those who have faith sacrifice freely for the Lord's work, and their acts of sacrifice increase their faith."[46] "The tests and trials of mortality are designed to determine whether men will use their time and talents in worldly or spiritual pursuits."[47] These tests include tests of the mind as much as any other tests. And the quest for rigorous scriptural evidence demands the dedication of time, the consecration of talents, and the willingness to be swallowed up in the Lord's purposes.

SOME PROBLEMS WITH EVIDENCE

Evidence may perform several useful functions, but this is not to say that evidence is some kind of panacea or elixir of pure knowledge. Evidence can even raise certain problems if it is not kept in proper balance.

Some people place too much weight on evidence. The scriptures caution against becoming overconfident or too secular. But such abuses are no different from anything else in life: riches may be abused, but that does not mean we stop working for a living; an artist runs the risk of pride, but that does not mean we cease improving our talents. As with all tools, the mind must be carefully used. Like a hammer, the intellect can be used either to build up or to tear down. Jesus gave us another analogy, that of a fruit tree, to help us determine the right balance: "By their fruits ye shall know them" (Matthew 7:20).

Other people go the opposite extreme and give too little attention to evidence and latch on to answers too readily. Brother Sperry once commented, "Too many persons in every generation, including our own, hope for things—fantastic things—in the name of faith and religion, but give little thought as to whether or not they are based on truth."[48]

Others halt between the two and become consumed by questions. It is a fact of life that we can ask more questions than can ever be answered. It takes skill and wisdom even to ask a good question. Sidney Sperry is a good example of a scholar who willingly addressed the so-called Isaiah question or the problem of the Sermon on the Mount in 3 Nephi. My work on these topics has not only satisfied all of my honest inquiries but has opened many unexpected insights. My study of the Sermon on the Mount as a temple text embedded in 3 Nephi 11–18 has elucidated the Book of Mormon beyond my most remote expectation and has turned what I saw as a potential problem into a great strength.[49]

THE "PROBLEM" OF PROOF

Of course, we cannot "prove" that the Book of Mormon or any other ultimate tenet of religious faith is true. Hugh Nibley has said, "The evidence that will prove or disprove the Book of Mormon does not exist."[50] Our desire is not to become some grand inquisitor, wanting to put other people over a barrel by producing undeniable reasons for belief that will convince the whole world and compel everyone to believe.[51] Since this is so, why should one bother to gather evidence or to do religious research at all?

In an ideal world, evidence would not be necessary. Things would be known directly, immediately, and certainly. The only problem is, we do not live in an ideal world, and it was not intended by God that we should so live. We are surrounded in this probationary state by possibilities, choices, and the need to seek and to work out our salvation with fear and trembling.

Moreover, in working with evidence, we must not forget what or who is really on trial. To quote President Benson: "The Book of Mormon is not on trial—the people of the world, including the members of the Church, are on trial as to what they will do with this second witness for Christ."[52] In the same way, when the world presumed to judge its Messiah to be a thing of naught, in reality the world was being judged: "He that believeth not is condemned already," says the Gospel of John, "and this is the condemnation, that light is come into the world, and men loved darkness rather than light" (John 3:18–19). As so often occurs, the gospel stands things on their heads: the weak are strong, the rich are poor, and the losers are the finders. And likewise, the testers are being tested. In dealing with and reacting to evidence, we actually reveal more about ourselves than we do about the subjects being tested, and we sharpen the sword not of human discernment but of divine judgment.

For this reason also we can understand why evidence does not affect all people in the same way. Not everyone will need evidences, and not all people will need them at every stage of their lives. Individuals see data differently, and "God made us free so to do."[53] In the end, it will always come down to the choice each person must make between believing the good or rejecting it. Abundant miraculous and physical evidence was given to Pharaoh, but he still rejected Jehovah. Evidence is the vehicle that makes the plan of choice and accountability viable. Without evidence both for and against two alternatives, no bona fide choice could ever be possible. Paraphrasing Lehi, we might add, Adam fell that men might choose; and evidence is that they might have a basis on which to choose.

FAITH, CHOICE, AND THE NATURE OF EVIDENCE

These theological observations about evidence invite a closer look at evidence itself. The better we understand both faith and evidence and the subjective elements that bridge the two, the better we will be able to bring them both beneficially together. Having seen how evidence contributes to faith, consider the elements of faith and the roles of personal choice in the nature of evidence and how evidence works.

People often misjudge the nature of evidence because, à la Perry Mason, they may take an overly simplistic view of evidence. The concept of evidence is complex. The power of evidence is shaped by metaphysical assumptions (such as causation) and cultural conditions (such as the value placed on proof), and it combines wide fields of human experience (including such philosophical concerns as epistemology, the reliability of sensory experience, the adequacy of language, the nature of history, and the psychology of persuasion).

The word *evidence* derives from the Latin *ex videns,* meaning anything which comes from *seeing* and also from *seeming*. Evidence is literally what meets the eye and, more than that, what seems to be from what we see. Evidence is based on hard facts, but even under the best of circumstances it works less automatically and more subjectively than many people realize. If evidence were not such a complicated matter, many things would be much simpler in our courtrooms, legislative sessions, and corporate board rooms as well as in our lecture halls and Gospel Doctrine classrooms.

Though this complexity may present problems in many cases, it also allows evidence to combine with faith, because in its complexity evidence is both a product of empirical data attractive to the mind amenable to study and the result of personal choices generated by the Spirit in faith. Not only is seeing believing but believing is seeing, as has been often said. Philosophical worldviews that would have it only one of these two ways offer us a model that limps on one leg.

In exploring the workings of evidence, I have found that the practice and study of law is a valuable experimental laboratory. Every legal case requires judges, lawyers, jurors, witnesses, and parties to define the issues, to organize evidence relevant to those issues, and to reach conclusions about the relative persuasiveness of the evidence. This wrenching world of legal experience—as problematic as it may seem to the general population after the advent of public television in the courtroom—is a furnace of realities that can teach us many things about the use and abuse of evidence. From these experiences, several operational rules emerge that illustrate the combination of objective and subjective elements in evidence, opening the way for one to add reason to one's faith and to engage faith in one's reason.

1. Any piece of evidence is deeply intertwined with a question. No real evidence exists until an issue is raised which that evidence tends to prove or disprove. By choosing what questions we will ask, we introduce a

subjective element into the inquiry—seeking and asking begin in faith. At the same time, our questions in turn determine what will become evidence—faith begins with asking and seeking.

Some questions are relatively simple and mostly objective: Where was Tom on the day of the crime? Other questions are more difficult and intermediate: What was Tom thinking? Ultimate questions frame the crux of the case and are largely subjective: Did Tom commit murder? Evidence may answer the simpler questions, but it rarely settles the ultimate issues. Judges and jurors adopt "findings of fact" and "conclusions of law" which are based on evidence, but those findings do not emerge spontaneously. They are separate, subjective formulations made by them in response to the evidence.

Similarly, we approach religious matters by asking different levels of questions. Certain queries ask ultimate questions: Did Joseph Smith tell the truth? Did Jesus appear to the Nephites? Such questions are usually tackled by breaking the question down and asking intermediate and easier questions: Is it reasonable to think that Lehi came from Jerusalem around 600 B.C.? Does it appear that many authors contributed to the writing of the Book of Mormon? To answer the intermediate questions, we start looking for specific bits of data. Was there timber in Arabia suitable for ship building? (Indeed there was.) In what style did the Jews write around 600 B.C.? (They used many varieties of parallelism.) In response to such evidence, we then voluntarily form our own "findings of fact," or opinions relative to the questions we have asked.

The study of chiasmus in the Book of Mormon illustrates in more detail this interaction of questions and data in the operation of evidence. One might ask: What does the presence of chiasmus in a text prove? Chiasmus is usually thought of as evidence of Hebrew style, which it is, but it may be evidence of many other things as well, depending fundamentally on what question a person asks. For example, is the English text of the Book of Mormon orderly, complex, precise and interestingly composed in purposeful units, or is it dull, chaotic, and redundant (as some have suggested)? Chiasmus gives evidence to answer that question. What is the meaning of a text? Form is often linked with content,[54] as in Alma 36, in which Alma meaningfully places the turning point in his life at the chiastic turning point of his beautiful chapter.[55] Were Book of Mormon authors well trained and careful in using their skills? Did they revise and rework their own earlier texts? The abrupt antithetical parallelisms in Mosiah 27:29–30 that were reworked into the chiastic pattern of Alma 36 offer internal evidence of the skill and care of these authors. Because all authors did not use chiasmus in the same ways, this literary element also provides evidence of multiple authorship and historical development in the Book of Mormon. King Benjamin is quite classical in his use of chiasmus. Alma the Younger is more creative and personal in his use of chiasmus.[56] Chiasmus also provides evidence that the Book of Mormon was translated from an underlying Hebrew text. In Helaman 6:10, for example, the chiastic turning point features the two words "Lord" and "Zedekiah" at the very center of this textual unit. The theophoric suffix at the end of the name Zedekiah, *–iah,* would in all probability have jumped out at the ancient reader as an obvious parallel to the Hebrew word for Lord. The chiasmus in Helaman 6 works even better in Hebrew than it does in English.[57] Chiasmus may further prove something about the precise nature of Joseph Smith's work as translator. Each time a word appears within these given frameworks, it seems to have been rendered by the same English word.

Each of these bits of evidence is interesting in its own

right, but these points do not begin to function as evidence until we have provided the question we seek to answer. Thus, we are involved in the inception and conception of evidence by the questions we choose to raise.

Some of the questions are simple, and objective answers to those questions from the realm of evidence may, to a large extent, confirm faith or make faith plausible. But the ultimate questions are more subjective, and although influenced by reason, their answers remain predominantly in the realm of belief.

2. Just about anything can serve potentially as evidence, depending on what a person wishes to emphasize. Some have viewed violent opposition to the Book of Mormon as evidence of its divinity.[58] Others see evidence of the same in its acceptance worldwide. Some rightly find evidence for the spiritual truthfulness of the Book of Mormon in its clarity, plainness, and expansiveness.[59] Others rightly find evidence for its miraculous origins in its complexity, subtlety, and precision. Some properly find persuasiveness in its uniformity and its conformity with eternal truths, whereas others appropriately find confirmation in its variety and cultural idiosyncracies.

When we seek evidence of something, we are prospecting, looking around at just about anything to see what we can find. Of course, not everything we find will ultimately amount to useful evidence, but just because some people may go overboard and wish to see every hole in the ground in South America as evidence of pre-Columbian baptismal fonts, that does not mean we should reject all evidence as worthless. Thomas Edison had several silly ideas before coming up with his many inventions.

3. For this reason, evidence can almost always be found or generated for and against just about any proposition. Only a very impoverished mind cannot find

evidence for just about anything he or she wants. Once again, this points out that evidence is not only discovered but also created. That creation is not arbitrarily *ex nihilo,* but neither is it impersonally predestined.

4. Different kinds of legal evidence evoke different kinds of responses. The law allows physical evidence, written documents, oral testimony, and so on. But at the same time, different people or legal situations may require or prefer to favor one kind of evidence over another. No rules automatically determine how one kind of evidence stacks up against another or what kind of evidence is best.

Many different types of evidence likewise exist for the Book of Mormon: internal and external, comparative and analytic, philological and doctrinal, statistical and thematical, chronological and cyclical, source critical (the seams between the texts abridged by Moroni in the book of Ether are still evident)[60] and literary. Its historical complexity and plausibility are supported by the study of warfare in the Book of Mormon (including remarkable coherence in its martial law, sacral ideology of war, and campaign strategy, buttressed by archaeological evidence regarding weaponry, armor, fortifications, and seasonality).[61] Evidence is found to enrich the prophetic allegory of Zenos by researching the horticulture of olives (it is evident that whoever wrote Jacob 5 had a high degree of knowledge about olives, which do not grow in New York).[62] Numerous legal practices in the Book of Mormon presuppose or make the best sense when understood against an ancient Israelite background. And so on, many times over. It objectively boggles the mind: How could any author keep all of these potential lines of evidence concurrently in his head while dictating the Book of Mormon without notes or a rough draft? It also subjectively engages the Spirit: How should all these different kinds of evidence be received, assessed, and evaluated?

5. Legal evidence is often circumstantial. The more direct the evidence, the more probative it usually is, and in some courts "circumstantial evidence only raises a probability."[63] But on the other hand, people may also choose to view circumstantial evidence as desirable and even necessary in certain situations. Indeed, the circumstances surrounding a particular event or statement are usually essential to understanding the matter. To quote Henry David Thoreau, "Some circumstantial evidence is very strong, as when you find a trout in the milk."[64] A dictum from the United States Supreme Court explains the power of circumstantial evidence: "Circumstantial evidence is often as convincing to the mind as direct testimony, and often more so. A number of concurrent facts, like rays of light, all converging to the same center, may throw not only a clear light but a burning conviction; a conviction of truth more infallible than the testimony even of two witnesses directly to a fact."[65] Accordingly, the convergence of huge amounts of circumstantial evidence, such as in the astonishingly short time in which the Book of Mormon was translated,[66] may be viewed quite favorably, if a person's spiritual disposition inclines one to receive and value such evidence.

6. Another fascinating and crucial question is, How are we to evaluate the cumulative weight of evidence? Some compilations of evidence are strong; other collections are weak. Yet once again, in most settings, no scale for evaluating the cumulative weight of evidence is readily available. No canons of method answer the question, How much evidence do we need in order to draw a certain conclusion? Answering this question is another choice that combines and bridges faith and evidence.

An interesting scale has developed in the law that prescribes specific levels of proof that are required to support certain legal results. The world of evidence is not black and white; there are many shades of gray. Ranging from a high degree of certitude on down, standards of proof on this spectrum include:

a. Beyond a reasonable doubt, dispositive, practically certain
b. Clear and convincing evidence, nearly certain
c. Competent and substantial evidence, well over half
d. Preponderance of evidence, more than half, more likely than not
e. Probable, as in probable cause, substantial possibility
f. Plausible, reasonably suspected
g. Material, relevant, merely possible.

Thus, for example, a person cannot be convicted of a first-degree murder unless the prosecution can prove its case "beyond a reasonable doubt." A civil case, however, between two contesting parties to a contract will be decided by a simple preponderance of the evidence. A grand jury can indict a person on probable cause.

But even within this spectrum, as helpful and sophisticated as it is, no precise definitions for these terms exist. Lawyers and judges still have only a feeling for what these legal terms mean, and their applications may vary from judge to judge. For example, a survey conducted in the Eastern District of New York among ten federal judges determined that the phrase "beyond a reasonable doubt" ranged from 76 percent to 95 percent certainty (although most were on the high end of this range). "Clear and convincing evidence" covered from 60 percent to 75 percent.[67] Obviously, a degree of subjectivity is again involved in deciding what level of certitude should be required or has been achieved in a given case.

In a religious setting, no arbiter prescribes or defines the level of evidence that will sustain a healthy faith. All individuals must set for themselves the levels of proof that they will require.[68] Yet how does one privately determine what burden of proof the Book of Mormon should bear? Should investigators require that it be proved beyond a reasonable doubt before experimenting with its words to learn of its truth or goodness? Should believers expect to have at least a preponderance of the evidence on their side in order to maintain their faith? Or is faith borne out sufficiently by a merely reasonable or plausible position, perhaps even in spite of all evidence? Few people realize how much rides on their personal choice in these matters and that their answer necessarily originates in the domain of faith.

7. Different legal cases call for different configurations of evidence. Some matters of common law or statute are what one might call single-factor cases: the presence or absence of a single factor is dispositive of the matter. More often, however, legal rules call for a number of elements that must be proved in order for a claim to be established. In such cases, every element is crucial, and each must be satisfied for the legal test to be met. In other cases, however, several criteria are recognized by law, none of which is absolutely essential, but, given the facts and circumstances of the particular case, may be indicative factors. Thus, for example, in determining whether a person is either an independent contractor or an employee, more than twenty factors have been recognized by law as being potentially significant in resolving the issue, but none of them is absolutely essential.[69]

Similarly, simple Book of Mormon evidences may come in all three of these configurations: the point of granting military exemption to the Ammonites but requiring them to "serve in the rear" by providing supplies compares readily with a single point of Jewish law;[70] the destruction of Ammonihah is consistent with the defined set of seven requirements found in the Israelite law of apostate cities (see Deuteronomy 13:12–16);[71]

evidence for Hebrew literary forms in the Book of Mormon is an open-ended accumulation.

In ultimate matters of faith, however, the individual must decide what configuration of evidence to require. Is the ultimate issue of Book of Mormon origins to be answered by a single-factor test, by satisfying the requirements of a multiple-element set (and if so, who defines what the essential elements are to be?), or by drawing on various facts and circumstances accumulated through spiritual experience and research? Individual choice on this matter will again affect how the objective evidence works in any given individual's mind and spirit.

8. In certain cases, the sum of the evidence may be greater than the total of its individual parts. "Pieces of evidence, each by itself insufficient, may together constitute a significant whole, and justify by their combined effect a conclusion."[72] The cumulative effect of evidence is in some ways perplexing, but again reflects the role of the observer's preference in how evidence works. Individual pieces of evidence, each of which standing alone is relatively insignificant and uninteresting, may take on vast importance in a person's mind as they combine to form a consistent pattern or coherent picture. It is in some senses ironic that a few strong single facts can be overwhelmed and defeated by a horde of true but less significant facts, a strategy I used in winning several tax cases. But should one give greater credence to a wide-ranging accumulation of assorted details or to a few single strong factors? Only personal judgment will answer that question.

9. Another interesting effect occurs when a good case is actually weakened by piling on a few weak additional points. A bad argument may be worse in some minds than no argument at all if the weak arguments tend to undermine confidence in the strong points. But who can tell what will work or not work for one person or

another? The degree of confidence a person is willing to place in any evidence is another manifestation of faith or personal response.

10. Similarly, advocacy and rhetoric are virtually part of the evidence. The techniques of presenting evidence are often as important as the evidence itself, and the subjective decision to feature certain points in favor of others can be the turning point of a case. Important facts forcefully presented take on added significance; crucial evidence overlooked and underused will not always even be noticed by the judge or jury.

Again, it is a sobering reality that the apparent victory in debates often goes to the witty, the clever, the articulate, and the overconfident. Hopefully, good arguments will always be presented in a clear manner so as not to obscure their true value; but because this does not always happen, prudent observers need to be careful to separate kernels of truth from the husks they are packaged in.

11. Not all evidence ultimately counts. In a court of law, the judge and jury will eventually decide to ignore some of the evidence, especially hearsay, mere opinions, or statistical probabilities. Similarly, in evaluating Book of Mormon evidence, one needs to be meticulous in separating fact from opinion. Likewise, fantastic statistics can be generated by either friends or foes of the book. This does not mean that statistical presentations should be ruled out of Book of Mormon discussions; some wordprinting studies, for example, have achieved noteworthy results.[73] But such evidence must not be exaggerated and must be approached with sophistication.

12. Constraints on time and the availability of witnesses or documentary evidence may be completely fortuitous yet also very important. If a witness is unavailable to testify in court, the case may be lost. Documentary evidence known or presumed once to

have existed is scarcely helpful. To reach a legal decision, time limitations are imposed on all parties; and in most cases, evidence discovered after a decision has become final is simply ignored.

In much the same way, important evidence relevant to religious matters will often be perpetually lacking. Thus, a person must subjectively choose at what point enough has been heard. Further historical or archaeological discoveries may eventually surface, but in the meantime, one must choose. In this regard, Elder LeGrand Richards counseled, "And when we find ourselves in conflict and confusion, we can well learn to wait a while for all the evidence and all the answers that now evade us."[74] And President Hugh B. Brown recommended: "With respect to some things that now seem difficult to understand, we can afford to wait until we have all the facts, until all the evidence is in. . . . If there seems to be conflict, it is because men, fallible men, are unable properly to interpret God's revelations or man's discoveries."[75]

THE NEED FOR CAUTION

Clearly, the matter of evidence is complex. While certain evidences will be demonstrably stronger and more objective than others, the processing of evidence is not simply a matter of feeding the data in one end of a machine and catching a conclusion as it falls out the other. Even in the law we read: "Absolute certainty and accuracy in fact-finding is an ideal, rather than an achievable goal."[76] Caution and care are in order.

Caution on the side of reason tells us that the power and value of evidence may be overrated in the world. Although evidence is certainly required to prevent our legal system of justice from degenerating into the Salem witch trials, even under the best of circumstances evidence is often ambiguous, incomplete, or nonexistent.

Caution is also advised on the side of faith. Revealed knowledge must be understood and interpreted correctly. What has actually been revealed? Do we know by revelation where the final battles in the Book of Mormon were fought? Do we know that because twenty-one chapters of Isaiah are quoted in the Book of Mormon that all sixty-six were on the plates of brass? Moreover, the implications of revelation are not always clear. Does the revealed fact that God is a God of order require us to reject the Heisenberg principle of uncertainty? Elder Widtsoe thought so. Perhaps that principle is only an expression of incomplete information, which will "disappear with increasing knowledge,"[77] but until we have further knowledge we must walk with caution in both spheres.

A PUZZLE

Maybe another metaphor will help—that of an old jigsaw puzzle. The picture on the box is a broad, or holistic, view of some reality given by revelation; but the picture on our box is incomplete (see Article of Faith 9) and unclear in spots (see 1 Corinthians 13:12). Moreover, we are also missing several pieces of the puzzle, and we are not even sure how many are gone. Some of the pieces in our box do not appear to belong to our puzzle at first, and others quite definitely are strays. The picture on the box becomes clearer to us, however, with greater study of its details. The more closely we examine the available pieces and the more use we make of our minds, the more we are able to put together a few pieces of solid truth here and there. We may, of course, put some of the pieces in the wrong place initially, but as other pieces are put into position and as we continually refer to the picture on the lid, we are able to correct those errors. As our understanding of both the picture and the pieces progresses, we gain greater respect for what we know, for how it all fits together, and for what we yet do not know.

From my study of Sidney B. Sperry, I think he would have liked the jigsaw puzzle analogy.[78] Brother Sperry always kept the big picture of revelation well in mind and was aware of the need to scrutinize the revelations closely. He was irresistibly drawn toward the challenge of putting the puzzle pieces together as far as he could, recognizing that "critical study and thought" was "necessary to understand [the Book of Mormon] completely,"[79] yet he remained well aware of the limitations of our knowledge and that we should be "on our guard against accepting too easily certain current theories."[80]

REDEEMING THE MIND

In the end, what we need is not a metaphor, but a metamorphosis. Metaphors strongly depict the paradigm, but only a shift of heart will make the difference if we are going to learn wisdom even by study and also by faith. How are we to foster both spirit and intellect? I have five suggestions.

First, be competent but resist pride. Joseph F. Smith firmly declared, "Of those who speak in his name, the Lord requires humility, not ignorance."[81] All are susceptible to the pervasive curse of pride, but scholars are above average in the pride category. We know by sad experience that when people get a little power, their natural disposition is to exercise unrighteous dominion, and clearly, knowledge is a form of power. Competence facilitates intellect, just as humility facilitates the Spirit.

Second, never oversimplify, and never overcomplicate. Truth is both simple and complex. The scriptures affirm both. The message of the gospel is simple, the way is clear, the path is straight; but the content of the gospel is also imponderable, inscrutable, and unfathomable.

Third, learn with a purpose, and then give purpose to

your learning. The bridge between faith and reason is purposeful activity. Study gives us facts, truth, and knowledge; faith gives us values, goodness, and objectives. Both are necessary. Knowledge, in and of itself, is morally neutral until it is put to work in support of some chosen purpose. There is a trouble with truth: Satan knows a lot of truth. He knows the laws of physics, physiology, psychology, and social behavior. What he lacks is the willingness to do what is good. That conviction comes through the light of Christ and with faith in Jesus. Without the love of Christ, truth is dangerous. No one, scholars included, operates above the moral law. I continue to be impressed in Alma 32 that what we learn when we plant the seed is not that the seed is true but that it is good. We should know that the gospel is both good and true, for our knowledge will "operate toward [our] salvation or condemnation as it is used or misused."[82]

Fourth, not only must we cultivate and listen to both intellect and spirit but we must apply the steps of repentance in overcoming our rebellious thoughts every bit as much as in rectifying our disobedient actions.[83] I find in the gospel a remarkable ability to harmonize and transcend such stubborn dichotomies as spirit and matter, rights and duties, and human and divine.[84] In no case is that power to unify more significant than in harmonizing the mind and the spirit. The only power that can achieve such unities is the power that truly makes one, the atonement of Jesus Christ. Our minds and our spirits both have need of the Atonement. A clean engine runs better, and so do a cleansed spirit and mind.

Perhaps it strikes you as odd to think of redeeming your mind. But is the human intellect any less or any more in need of redemption than any other part of the soul? Is a mortal's mind any less subject to the Fall than the body? Mind and spirit are polarized only when both are unredeemed. The natural mind is an enemy to God, but through the redeeming powers of the atonement of Christ, the human spirit and the human intellect both become mutually cooperative counterparts as they work in harmony with the mind and will of God.

So, the question becomes, Has our thinking been redeemed? Have our mind and spirit both been sanctified by the atoning blood of Christ? Has the finger of the Lord touched our inert cerebral stones and made them into light-giving gems? Have you been "transformed by the renewing of your mind"? (Romans 12:2). Has your mind yielded "to the enticings of the Holy Spirit, and . . . [become] as a child, submissive, meek, humble, patient, full of love, willing to submit to all things which the Lord seeth fit to inflict"? (Mosiah 3:19). Elder Maxwell has said, "Absolute truth calls for absolute love and absolute patience."[85] The qualities mentioned by King Benjamin in Mosiah apply as much to the mind as to anything else. The basic meaning of the word *atonement* in Greek is to reconcile two alienated parties.[86] It can fully reconcile the tensions between reason and revelation not by obliterating the distinctiveness between reasoned thought and heartfelt spiritual experience but by bringing both into oneness in Christ.

Finally, seek the fulness. What we seek in the dispensation of the fulness of times is the fulness of the everlasting gospel, not just one half or the other of the loaf of the bread of life. Longing to pour out upon the Saints more of what he knew, Joseph Smith once remarked, "It is my meditation all the day, and more than my meat and drink, to know how I shall make the Saints of God comprehend the visions that roll like an overflowing surge before my mind."[87] Brother Nibley has similarly said, "Our search for knowledge should be ceaseless, which means that it is open-ended. . . . True knowledge never shuts the door on more knowledge, but zeal often does"; Adam and Abraham had "far greater and more truth than what we have, and yet the particular genius of each was that he was constantly 'seeking for *greater* light and knowledge.'"[88] We are not likely to have the kind of faith it will take to receive all that the Father has if we have not served him with all that we do have, that is with all our heart, might, mind, and strength.

THE CHOICE IS OURS

"Of all our needs," President Gordon B. Hinckley has said, "the greatest is an increase in faith."[89] Anything that truly helps in that process, even a little bit, should be useful to us.

As a young man and still today, I have always felt very satisfied in my testimony of the Book of Mormon. At first, I believed that the book was true with little or no evidence of any kind at all. Never expecting to find great proofs or evidence for the book, I have been astonished by what the Lord has done. In all of this, I have not been disappointed but richly satisfied.

It seems clear enough that the Lord does not intend for the Book of Mormon to be an open-and-shut case intellectually, either pro or con. If God had intended that, he could have left more concrete evidences one way or the other. Instead, it seems that the Lord has maintained a careful balance between requiring us to exercise faith and allowing us to find reasons that affirm the stated origins of this record. The choice is then entirely ours. Ultimately, evidences may not be that important; but then it is easy to say that the airplane or the parachute has become irrelevant after you are safely on the ground.

We are blessed to have the Book of Mormon. It is the word of God. It would be ideal if all could accept it without suspicion and then, upon humble prayer, receive the witness of the Holy Ghost that it is true, but in this less than ideal world, it is good that so much evidence can bring us to believe and help us to nurture faith in this extraordinary book.

Because of my study of this book, I find myself drawn closer to the Lord. I am grateful as this deepening relationship enriches the love I feel for this precious record. Gratefully, as my knowledge about this book grows, my faith grows, too.

NOTES

1. See, for example, Henry B. Eyring, ed., *On Being a Disciple-Scholar* (Salt Lake City: Bookcraft, 1995); Robert L. Millet, ed., *"To Be Learned Is Good If . . ."* (Salt Lake City: Bookcraft, 1987).

2. Gordon B. Hinckley, *Faith: The Essence of True Religion* (Salt Lake City: Deseret Book, 1989), 73.

3. Neal A. Maxwell, *Deposition of a Disciple* (Salt Lake City: Deseret Book, 1976), 15.

4. Neal A. Maxwell, "The Disciple-Scholar," in Henry B. Eyring, ed., *On Being a Disciple-Scholar* (Salt Lake City: Bookcraft, 1995), 3.

5. Boyd K. Packer, "'I Say unto You, Be One' (D&C 38:27)," *Brigham Young University 1990–91 Devotionals and Fireside Speeches* (Provo: Brigham Young University, 1991), 89.

6. Used by Lowell L. Bennion, "The Uses of the Mind in Religion," *BYU Studies* 14, no. 1 (1973): 47–55, arguing that one cannot turn one's back on either the religious (biblical) or the rational (Greek) tradition, 48.

7. Truman G. Madsen, "Philosophy," in B. H. Roberts, *The Truth, the Way, the Life,* ed. John W. Welch (Provo: BYU Studies, 1994), lxxiii.

8. See, generally, Elisabeth Koffmahn, *Die Doppelurkunden aus der Wüste Juda* (Leiden: Brill, 1968); Leopold Fischer, "Die Urkunden in Jer 31 11–14 nach den Ausgrabungen und dem Talmud," *Zeitschrift der Altertums Wissenschaft* 30 (1910): 136–42; Leopold Wenger, "Über Stempel und Siegel," *Zeitschrift der Savigny-Stiftung* 42 (1921): 611–38.

9. Von Domaszewski, "Ein neues Militärdiplom," *Die Altertümer unserer heidnischen Vorzeit* 5, no. 4 (1911): 181–86, Tafel 33, published by the Römisch-germanischen Zentralmuseum in Mainz.

10. John W. Welch, ed., *Reexploring the Book of Mormon* (Salt Lake City: Deseret Book and FARMS, 1992), 248–49.

11. Welch, *Reexploring the Book of Mormon,* 64–65.

12. John W. Welch, "Words and Phrases in Jacob 5," in Stephen D. Ricks and John W. Welch, eds., *The Allegory of the Olive Tree* (Salt Lake

City: Deseret Book and FARMS, 1994), 176.

13. Sidney B. Sperry, "Types of Literature in the Book of Mormon: The American Gospel, Epistles, Psalms, Lamentations, Historical Narrative, Memoir, Prophetic Discourse, Oratory, Patriarchal Blessings, Symbolic Prophecy, Prophetic Narrative, Prophetic Dialogue, Allegories, Prayers, Songs, Genealogies," *Journal of Book of Mormon Studies* 4, no. 1 (1995): 48–118.

14. Sidney B. Sperry, "The Book of Mormon As Translation English," *Journal of Book of Mormon Studies* 4, no. 1 (1995): 210.

15. Sperry, "The Book of Mormon As Translation English," 214.

16. Sidney B. Sperry, "Hebrew Idioms in the Book of Mormon," *Journal of Book of Mormon Studies* 4, no. 1 (1995): 225.

17. "The Lord does not convince men of his truth by placing before their eyes and in their hands tangible evidence, as a lawyer may do before the court, marking it exhibit A and exhibit B, and then expect it to be accepted. The Lord expects the searcher after truth to approach him with a contrite spirit and with sincerity of purpose, if he will do this and keep the commandments of the Lord, he shall receive the witness through the Holy Spirit and shall know the truth." Joseph Fielding Smith, *Doctrines of Salvation,* 3 vols. (Salt Lake City: Bookcraft, 1954–56), 3:228.

18. Joseph Smith, *Teachings of the Prophet Joseph Smith,* sel. Joseph Fielding Smith (Salt Lake City: Deseret Book, 1938), 267.

19. John A. Widtsoe, *Evidences and Reconciliations,* 3d ed. (Salt Lake City: Bookcraft, 1943), 28.

20. Widtsoe, *Evidences and Reconciliations,* 29.

21. Smith, *Doctrines of Salvation,* 2:124.

22. Maxwell, *Deposition of a Disciple,* 16.

23. Hinckley, *Faith,* 10.

24. Maxwell, *Deposition of a Disciple,* 49.

25. John L. Sorenson, *An Ancient American Setting for the Book of Mormon* (Salt Lake City: Deseret Book and FARMS, 1985), 111 and fn. 16.

26. Welch, *Reexploring the Book of Mormon,* 41–43.

27. Welch, *Reexploring the Book of Mormon,* 250–52.

28. Austin Farrar, "Grete Clerk," in Jocelyn Gibb, comp., *Light on C. S. Lewis* (New York: Harcourt and Brace, 1965), 26; cited in Neal A. Maxwell, "Discipleship and Scholarship," *BYU Studies* 32, no. 3 (Summer 1992): 5.

29. Maxwell, "Discipleship and Scholarship," 5.

30. Susan Easton Black, *Finding Christ through the Book of Mormon* (Salt Lake City: Deseret Book, 1987).

31. John W. Welch, "Ten Testimonies of Jesus Christ from the Book of Mormon," in Bruce A. Van Orden and Brent L. Top, eds., *Doctrines of the Book of Mormon* (Salt Lake City: Deseret Book, 1992), 223–42.

32. Maxwell, *Deposition of a Disciple,* 49. Elder Maxwell has enumerated a lengthy list of evidences that raise "vexing challenges for disbelievers and critics who reject the true account but remain surrounded by increasing incredibilia." Neal A. Maxwell, "The Ends of the Earth Shall Inquire after Thy Name," address delivered at the Missionary Training Center, Provo, Utah, 23 Aug. 1994.

33. Jeffrey R. Holland, "A Standard unto My People," address delivered at CES Symposium, Brigham Young University, Provo, Utah, 9 Aug. 1994 (Provo: FARMS, 1994), 7.

34. Stephen L Richards, in Conference Report, Oct. 1954, 96.

35. Hinckley, *Faith,* 78.

36. John W. Welch, "Legal Perspectives on the Slaying of Laban," *Journal of Book of Mormon Studies* 1, no. 1 (1992): 119–41.

37. John W. Welch, "The Temple in the Book of Mormon," in Donald W. Parry, ed., *Temples of the Ancient World* (Salt Lake City: Deseret Book, 1994), 353–55.

38. John W. Welch, "A Book You Can Respect," *Ensign* 7 (September 1977): 45–48.

39. B. H. Roberts, *Deseret News,* 11 Oct. 1930.

40. Bruce R. McConkie, *A New Witness for the Articles of Faith* (Salt Lake City: Deseret Book, 1985), 466.

41. McConkie, *New Witness,* 466.

42. B. H. Roberts, *New Witnesses for God,* 3 vols. (Salt Lake City: Deseret Book, 1909), 2:vi–vii.

43. Roberts, *New Witnesses for God,* 2:vii; cited by Ted E. Brewerton in Conference Report, Oct. 1995, 39; or *Ensign* 25 (November 1995): 31.

44. Roberts, *New Witnesses for God,* 2:vii.

45. Hinckley, *Faith,* 5.

46. McConkie, *New Witness,* 189.

47. McConkie, *New Witness,* 188.

48. Sidney B. Sperry, "Some Universals in the Book of Mormon," *Journal of Book of Mormon Studies* 4, no. 1 (1995): 232.

49. John W. Welch, *The Sermon at the Temple and the Sermon on the Mount* (Salt Lake City: Deseret Book and FARMS, 1990).

50. Hugh W. Nibley, *Since Cumorah* (Salt Lake City: Deseret Book, 1967), viii; see also *The Collected Works of Hugh Nibley* (Salt Lake City: Deseret Book and FARMS, 1987), 7:xiv.

51. Richard L. Bushman, "My Belief," *BYU Studies* 25, no. 2 (1985): 23–30. Bushman rightly learned that such expectations are unrealistic (28–29); but there are other alternatives besides discarding all evidence as "essentially irrelevant" (30).

52. Ezra Taft Benson, in Conference Report, Oct. 1984, 7; or *Ensign* 14 (November 1984): 8.

53. Maxwell, *Deposition of a Disciple,* 18.

54. In Mosiah 5:10–12, for example, King Benjamin is interested in contrasting those who remember the covenantal name and those who do not. The structure of the chiasm in this text accentuates this sharp contrast, the either/or separating the two options. In Alma 41:13–15, the balanced sense of divine justice, which will reward good for that which is good, and righteous for that which is righteous, is conveyed subtly by the balance implicit in its literary structure. A similar effect is achieved in Leviticus 24, where the "bruise for bruise, eye for eye" sense of talionic justice is reflected perfectly in the chiastic structure that embraces that content. John W. Welch, "Chiasmus in Biblical Law," *Jewish Law Association Studies IV: The Boston Conference Volume,* ed. Bernard Jackson (Atlanta: Scholars Press, 1990), 5–22, esp. 7–11.

55. John W. Welch, "Alma 36: A Masterpiece," in *Rediscovering the Book of Mormon,* ed. John L. Sorenson and Melvin J. Thorne (Salt Lake City: Deseret Book and FARMS, 1991), 114–31.

56. The pair of lists that is inverted to become a list of pairs in the opposite order in Alma 41:13–15 is brilliantly creative.

57. John W. Welch, "Chiasmus in Helaman 6:7–13" (Provo: FARMS, 1987); see also Welch, *Reexploring the Book of Mormon,* 230–32.

58. McConkie, *New Witness,* 462.

59. McConkie, *New Witness,* 467.

60. John W. Welch, "Preliminary Comments on the Sources behind the Book of Ether" (Provo: FARMS, 1986).

61. William J. Hamblin and Stephen D. Ricks, eds., *Warfare in the Book of Mormon* (Salt Lake City: Deseret Book, 1990).

62. Ricks and Welch, *Allegory of the Olive Tree,* 484–562.

63. *Reg. v. Rowton* (1865), 13 W.R. 437; cited in Norton-Kyshe, *Dictionary of Legal Quotations,* 88.

64. Henry David Thoreau, *Journal,* 11 Nov. 1850; cited in Angela Partington, ed., *The Oxford Dictionary of Quotations* (Oxford: Oxford University Press, 1992), 696.

65. *Thompson v. Bowle,* 71 U.S. (4 Wall.) 463, 473 (1867); cited in Eugene C. Gerhart, ed., *Quote It! Memorable Legal Quotations* (New York: Boardman, 1969), 205.

66. John W. Welch and Tim Rathbone, "The Translation of the Book of Mormon: Basic Historical Information" (Provo: FARMS, 1986).

67. *United States v. Fatico,* 458 Federal Supplement 388, 410 (Eastern District of New York, 1978). See also Timothy J. Martens, "The Standard of Proof for Preliminary Questions of Fact under the Fourth and Fifth Amendments," *Arizona Law Review* 30 (1988): 119–33.

68. Elder Widtsoe felt that "the weight of evidence" on one side or the other was sufficient to remove all doubt. Widtsoe, *Evidences and Reconciliations,* 28. Joseph Fielding Smith asserted that the highest standard of proof could be met, that evidence "prove[d] beyond the possibility of doubt that Joseph Smith and Oliver Cowdery spoke the truth." Smith, *Doctrines of Salvation,* 2:124.

69. Revenue Ruling 87–41, 1987–1 Cumulative Bulletin 296.

70. Welch, *Reexploring the Book of Mormon,* 191.

71. Welch, *Reexploring the Book of Mormon,* 176–79.

72. Lord Wright, in *Grant v. Australian Knitting Mills, Ltd.,* A. C. (1936) 85, 96; cited in M. Frances McNamara, ed., *2,000 Classic Legal Quotations* (Rochester, New York: Lawyers Cooperative, 1992), 207.

73. John L. Hilton, "On Verifying Wordprint Studies: Book of Mormon Authorship," *BYU Studies* 30 (1990): 89–108.

74. LeGrand Richards, in Conference Report, Oct. 1952, 96.

75. Hugh B. Brown, in Conference Report, Apr. 1955, 82.

76. Perry Meyer, "Evidence in the Future," *Canadian Bar Journal* 51 (1973): 118.

77. Widtsoe, *Evidences and Reconciliations,* 13. "Chance, disorder, chaos are ruled out of the physical universe." 13.

78. Members of the Sperry family and former colleagues of his confirmed this point after my presentation of this paper at the Sperry Symposium on 7 October 1995. Sidney Sperry was an avid puzzle solver and even won prizes in national puzzle contests.

79. Sidney B. Sperry, "The Book of Mormon and the Problem of the Pentateuch," *Journal of Book of Mormon Studies* 4, no. 1 (1995): 124.

80. Sperry, "Types of Literature in the Book of Mormon," 62.

81. Joseph F. Smith, *Gospel Doctrine* (Salt Lake City: Deseret Book, 1919), 206.

82. Smith, *Gospel Doctrine,* 206, citing *Juvenile Instructor* 41 (August 1906): 465.

83. Indeed, the word for *repentance* in Greek, *metanoia,* means literally to change one's mind.

84. John W. Welch, "BYU Studies: Into the 1990s," *Brigham Young University Studies* 31, no. 4 (1991): 25.

85. Maxwell, *Deposition of a Disciple,* 17.

86. Gerhard Kittel, ed., *Theological Dictionary of the New Testament,* 10 vols. (Grand Rapids, Mich.: Eerdmans, 1964), 1:255, 258. See also Hugh W. Nibley, "The Meaning of the Atonement," in *Approaching Zion* (Salt Lake City: Deseret Book and FARMS, 1989), 556, 560–61, vol 9. of *The Collected Works of Hugh Nibley.*

87. Smith, *Teachings of the Prophet Joseph Smith,* 296.

88. Nibley, *Approaching Zion,* 70–71.

89. Gordon B. Hinckley, in Conference Report, Oct. 1987, 68; or *Ensign* 17 (November 1987): 54.

INDEX